93

BARRON'S BOOK NOTES

ERNEST HEMINGWAY'S
The Old Man and the Sea

BY
Jim Auer

SERIES EDITOR
Michael Spring
Editor, *Literary Cavalcade*
Scholastic Inc.

D1318639

BARRON'S

BARRON'S EDUCATIONAL SERIES, INC.

ACKNOWLEDGMENTS

We would like to acknowledge the many painstaking hours of work Holly Hughes and Thomas F. Hirsch have devoted to making the *Book Notes* series a success.

© Copyright 1984 by Barron's Educational Series, Inc.

All rights reserved.
No part of this book may be reproduced in any form, by photostat, microfilm, xerography, or any other means, or incorporated into any information retrieval system, electronic or mechanical, without the written permission of the copyright owner.

All inquiries should be addressed to:
Barron's Educational Series, Inc.
250 Wireless Boulevard
Hauppauge, New York 11788

Library of Congress Catalog Card No. 84-18527

International Standard Book No. 0-8120-3432-5

Library of Congress Cataloging in Publication Data
Auer, Jim.
 Ernest Hemingway's The old man and the sea.

 (Barron's book notes)
 Bibliography: p. 101
 Summary: A guide to reading "The Old Man and the Sea" with a critical and appreciative mind. Includes background on the author's life and times, sample tests, term paper suggestions, and a reading list.
 1. Hemingway, Ernest, 1899–1961. Old man and the sea.
 [1. Hemingway, Ernest, 1899–1961. Old man and the sea.
 2. American literature—History and criticism] I. Title.
 PS3515.E370513 1984   813'.52   84-18527
 ISBN 0-8120-3432-5 (pbk.)

PRINTED IN THE UNITED STATES OF AMERICA

456   550   987654

CONTENTS

ADVISORY BOARD

We wish to thank the following educators who helped us focus our *Book Notes* series to meet student needs and critiqued our manuscripts to provide quality materials.

Murray Bromberg, Principal
Wang High School of Queens, Holliswood, New York

Sandra Dunn, English Teacher
Hempstead High School, Hempstead, New York

Lawrence J. Epstein, Associate Professor of English
Suffolk County Community College, Selden, New York

Leonard Gardner, Lecturer, English Department
State University of New York at Stony Brook

Beverly A. Haley, Member, Advisory Committee
National Council of Teachers of English Student
Guide Series, Fort Morgan, Colorado

Elaine C. Johnson, English Teacher
Tamalpais Union High School District
Mill Valley, California

Marvin J. LaHood, Professor of English
State University of New York College at Buffalo

Robert Lecker, Associate Professor of English
McGill University, Montréal, Québec, Canada

David E. Manly, Professor of Educational Studies
State University of New York College at Geneseo

Bruce Miller, Associate Professor of Education
State University of New York at Buffalo

Frank O'Hare, Professor of English
Ohio State University, Columbus, Ohio

Faith Z. Schullstrom, Member, Executive Committee
National Council of Teachers of English
Director of Curriculum and Instruction
Guilderland Central School District, New York

Mattie C. Williams, Director, Bureau of Language Arts
Chicago Public Schools, Chicago, Illinois

HOW TO USE THIS BOOK

You have to know how to approach literature in order to get the most out of it. This *Barron's Book Notes* volume follows a plan based on methods used by some of the best students to read a work of literature.

Begin with the guide's section on the author's life and times. As you read, try to form a clear picture of the author's personality, circumstances, and motives for writing the work. This background usually will make it easier for you to hear the author's tone of voice, and follow where the author is heading.

Then go over the rest of the introductory material—such sections as those on the plot, characters, setting, themes, and style of the work. Underline, or write down in your notebook, particular things to watch for, such as contrasts between characters and repeated literary devices. At this point, you may want to develop a system of symbols to use in marking your text as you read. (Of course, you should only mark up a book you own, not one that belongs to another person or a school.) Perhaps you will want to use a different letter for each character's name, a different number for each major theme of the book, a different color for each important symbol or literary device. Be prepared to mark up the pages of your book as you read. Put your marks in the margins so you can find them again easily.

Now comes the moment you've been waiting for—the time to start reading the work of literature. You may want to put aside your *Barron's Book Notes* volume until you've read the work all the way through. Or you may want to alternate, reading the *Book Notes* analysis of each section as soon as you have finished reading the corresponding part of the original. Before you move on, reread crucial passages you don't fully understand. (Don't take this guide's analysis for granted—make up your own mind as to what the work means.)

Once you've finished the whole work of literature, you may want to review it right away, so you can firm up your ideas about what it means. You may want to leaf through the book concentrating on passages you marked in reference to one character or one theme. This is also a good time to reread the *Book Notes* introductory material, which pulls together insights on specific topics.

When it comes time to prepare for a test or to write a paper, you'll already have formed ideas about the work. You'll be able to go back through it, refreshing your memory as to the author's exact words and perspective, so that you can support your opinions with evidence drawn straight from the work. Patterns will emerge, and ideas will fall into place; your essay question or term paper will almost write itself. Give yourself a dry run with one of the sample tests in the guide. These tests present both multiple-choice and essay questions. An accompanying section gives answers to the multiple-choice questions as well as suggestions for writing the essays. If you have to select a term paper topic, you may choose one from the list of suggestions in this book. This guide also provides you with a reading list, to help you when you start research for a term paper, and a selection of provocative comments by critics, to spark your thinking before you write.

THE AUTHOR
AND HIS TIMES

Autumn, 1952. *The Old Man and the Sea* is first published in an issue of *Life* magazine. Within 48 hours, 5,318,650 copies are sold. The American book edition sells 50,000 copies in advance, the British edition 20,000. Critics go wild. The public practically worships this rugged bearded author who combines the images of "grandfather" and "sea captain."

1953. Ernest Hemingway receives the Pulitzer Prize for *The Old Man and the Sea.*

1954. Hemingway receives the Nobel Prize for literature, the greatest formal international award a writer can receive. The award specifically mentions *The Old Man and the Sea.*

July 2, 1961. Sunday morning. Hemingway awakens early at his home in secluded Ketchum, Idaho. He loads a double-barreled shotgun, places the butt against the floor and the barrels against his forehead, and pulls the trigger.

There's a sizable list of famous people who have ended their own lives. Occasionally someone who commits suicide will leave a brief note, but often we're left guessing at the reasons.

Ernest Hemingway didn't leave a suicide note, yet he did leave behind many statements about life—by means of the characters he created in his stories. His "old man" is certainly one of them, perhaps the main one. You may or may not see a connection between Hemingway's old man and Hemingway's decision to end it all on July 2, 1961. But the possibility is certainly there.

Hemingway's nearly sixty-two years make an interesting story by themselves. But they're even more interesting in the light of this "little" story of an old Cuban fisherman and his three-day battle with a huge fish. The old man, Santiago, experiences battle, rejection, failure, loss, glory, and triumph. In his life, Hemingway did too.

Does this mean the old man of the story *is* Hemingway? Was he saying, "Here is a shortened, symbolic representation of my life"? Although some critics would agree, Hemingway himself did not encourage this view. You can enjoy speculating on this issue. But there's an old saying, "Every piece of writing is at least a little bit autobiographical." In this case it's probably true.

Keep those ideas in mind: battle, rejection, failure, loss, glory, and triumph. Look for them in major events or periods of Hemingway's life. And then look for them in *The Old Man and the Sea*.

For someone who lived his adult life in bold, often brawny fashion across three continents in full public view, his early years were rather serene ones in a quiet town. Hemingway was born on July 21, 1899, in Oak Park, Illinois. As a boy he became a very good fisherman and hunter at the family's summer cottage in Michigan. These adventures were his fondest boyhood memories.

His mother was very inclined toward the arts, especially music. Young Ernest received voice and cello lessons, which he was supposed to practice in the actual "music room" of their large home. When she was out, he would push the musical paraphernalia to the side of the room and use it as a boxing arena with his friends.

A relatively minor rebellion. But it suggests the individualism which Hemingway's later life was to demonstrate on a larger scale.

The individualism blossomed when he graduated from high school and showed no interest in college, even though he had been a good student. In fact, he stubbornly refused college.

This individualism is another idea to keep in mind when you relate Hemingway's life to *The Old Man and the Sea*. The old man Santiago isn't exactly a groupie either. In fact, early in the story, the boy Manolin tells Santiago, "But there is only you." Most people would agree there was only one Hemingway and perhaps add that there will never be another remotely like him.

Hemingway was interested not in college but in war. World War I had been raging for three years when Hemingway carried his high school diploma back down the aisle, and he was determined to participate before the action stopped.

But he met rejection. First, his father refused to let him enlist. Later, when his father gave permission, the armed forces rejected him because of poor sight in one eye.

Still he did get some experience of violence, if not of actual war. He got a job as a cub reporter with the Kansas City *Star* covering the police and hospital stories.

Finally he managed to get his taste of war. More than a taste. Enlisting with the Italian Red Cross as an ambulance driver, he made his way to the front lines. During a furious Austrian shelling of the Italian troops, he carried a wounded soldier to safety. And while he carried the soldier in his arms, he was struck by two hundred pieces of shrapnel from a mortar shell and received multiple wounds from machine gun bullets.

Though it was an extraordinary act, why did he put himself in such danger? One explanation would be that he simply acted from instinct, hardly thinking. Another is that he deliberately did it because it was "what a man must do."

This is another good incident to keep in mind when you analyze the old man out on the sea, facing his great challenge. Does Santiago act as he does simply from instinct, because he doesn't know any better? Or does he consciously embrace the challenge and its pain—aware that he might not survive?

There was a moment of glory for Hemingway's act of military heroism: a decoration from the Italian government and some glowing stories in his hometown papers. And a moment of rejection: the American nurse he fell in love with while recovering turned down his proposal of marriage.

The glory of his hero's welcome back in the States didn't last either. He was now determined to be a writer, but his articles and stories were rejected by one magazine after another.

His "doing nothing" brought the disapproval of his parents, who felt their son was loafing instead of working. Hemingway's "birthday present" at age twenty-one was a Get-Out-Of-The-House-Until-You-Grow-Up-And-Get-A-Real-Job letter which his mother personally handed to him.

He did get out and find a real job, married a girl named Hadley Richardson, and moved to Paris as correspondent for the Toronto *Star*. His newspaper work succeeded. His other literary attempts, the ones that really mattered to him, didn't. He kept submitting manuscripts. They kept getting rejected.

He had hopes for the manuscripts, though. Every writer has hopes for unsold manuscripts which he or she intends to revise, resubmit, and finally sell. But in December of 1923, a suitcase containing almost everything he had written, originals and carbons, was stolen and never recovered. All the material from which he hoped to build literary and financial success—wiped out.

Could there be a connection between Hemingway's suitcase and Santiago's marlin? The marlin was "a fish to keep a man all winter." It's another interesting speculation based on the premise that all writing is at least partially autobiographical.

Yet success came shortly afterward. In 1925 a book of short stories entitled *In Our Time* was published; in 1926, a novel, *The Sun Also Rises;* in 1928 another story collection, *Men Without Women.* All of these books were well received by the critics and by the public.

There were exceptions. Hemingway's parents found their son's writing distasteful, even shocking. Hemingway's characters were not always genteel people with polite speech habits. Dr. and Mrs. Hemingway found this offensive and even returned their copies of *In Our Time* to the publisher. And 1927 saw Hemingway's divorce from Hadley, an action which further outraged his parents.

His life became, for a while, a rather bumpy ride between positive and negative, fortune and reversal. There was a happy wedding to Pauline Pfeiffer later in 1927 and in 1928 a warm reconciliation with his family. But in December of 1928, Hemingway's father gave in to a period of growing depression and shot himself with a revolver.

"Just when you have it, you lose it." "Life is a mixed bag." You've probably heard statements like these. It's certainly not difficult to see these themes in

The Old Man and the Sea. Santiago's mixed bag of triumph and tragedy certainly has a precedent in the life of Hemingway, his creator.

Hemingway moved to Key West, Florida, poured himself into writing, and a year later produced *A Farewell to Arms*, a novel which raised him to the very peak of literary and financial success at the age of thirty—gratifying to a writer who began his career collecting rejection slips.

Hemingway filled the next several years satisfying his desire for broader and deeper experiences. He reveled in deep-sea fishing off the Florida Keys; he hunted big game in Wyoming. In the summer of 1933 he undertook an African safari but contracted amoebic dysentery on the way.

So, like Santiago, he played out his great adventure weak and hurting. Others told him to go back, postpone the hunt, wait until he recovered. Hemingway said no. In terms of game, the safari was successful. In spite of his condition, he shot and dropped a charging Cape buffalo a few feet before the enraged animal would have killed him.

A few feet closer, a few seconds later, and there would have been no old man, Santiago. But Hemingway's whole life and outlook suggest that, if he had known in advance of this deadly possibility, he would have embraced it even more enthusiastically, just as Santiago certainly knew there was great danger in going far out beyond the normal fishing waters.

Hemingway's fascination with war occupied him again from 1936 to 1938 in Spain. This is a strange side of his life. He absolutely loved being *in* a war; the closer to the most heated action, the better. Then, when it was over, he would write about the futility and horror of war.

He covered the Spanish Civil War as a correspondent, following the Loyalist infantry into the fiercest battles. He was thoroughly depressed when they were finally defeated by the Franco forces.

From this experience came *For Whom the Bell Tolls*, in 1940. Paramount Pictures bought the film rights for $150,000—an astronomical figure in the early 40s. Hemingway was now in a position to call his own shots; he sold the film rights only after Paramount agreed to his insistence that Gary Cooper and Ingrid Bergman play the lead roles.

The second marriage had ended in divorce in 1938. In 1941 he married Martha Gellhorn. They lived on an estate outside Havana, Cuba, surrounded by luxuries. Nearby was a small fishing village.

World War II, as other wars before it, captivated Hemingway. Again deciding to be a correspondent, he became chief of *Collier's* European bureau. He accompanied the Royal Air Force on several bombing raids over occupied France; he crossed the English Channel with American troops on June 6, 1944. Again he was in the thick of fighting in Belgium and Germany, sending back stirring accounts of the battlefield.

In 1945 his third marriage broke up; in 1946 his fourth, and lasting, marriage to Mary Welsh began. They resettled at the estate outside Havana, where Hemingway was now an international celebrity.

But again, "Just when you have it . . ." 1950 brought professional disaster, at least in terms of critical opinion. His book *Across the River and Into the Trees* received biting, almost vicious reviews. Ernest Hemingway appeared to be washed up as a writer.

Then in 1952 came *The Old Man and the Sea*. And the Pulitzer. And the Nobel. It was his last major work published while he was still alive. (Two books, *A Moveable Feast* and *Islands in the Stream*, have been published since his death.)

And in 1961 came the end of it all—by his own hand. His health had been deteriorating. Nothing, including visits to the famous Mayo Clinic, seemed able to return him to the masculine vigor he so enjoyed. Did he decide that if he could not "do it all" he would prefer to do nothing?

In any case, his great adventure with life and literature was ended, by his own choosing. And here we have a definite difference between the conclusion of *The Old Man and the Sea* and the conclusion of Hemingway's own life.

Santiago is weak and hurting. He is perhaps sicker than he knows. But he and Manolin make plans to fish together again, to undertake perhaps another attempt to bring back the big one.

Hemingway himself chose not to.

THE NOVEL

The Plot

Compared to most novels, *The Old Man and the Sea* is unusual in many ways. The time span is very short; most of the action occurs during three days and three nights on the sea. There are also a "day before" and part of a "day after." Consider the demands this makes on the writer. Three days in the life of one person—with no other people around. Normally that would make a *very* boring story. But most readers agree that *The Old Man and the Sea* is not boring. How did Hemingway make this tiny time span in the life of only one person interesting?

The Day Before   Santiago, the "old man," has gone eighty-four days without catching a fish. He's a widower and there's no mention of any children of his own. He has only "the boy," Manolin, as companion and genuine friend. Manolin had been Santiago's apprentice, but the boy's parents have made him work on another fishing boat because Santiago has "bad luck." But he's still loyal to Santiago and helps the old man prepare for an attempt to catch "the big one."

The First Day   Santiago rows his skiff out from the Havana harbor far beyond normal fishing waters, hoping to end his string of bad luck with a really huge catch. He sets his lines and reads the signs of the sea, finding them favorable.

His deepest line shows signs of a fish nibbling at the bait, and he can tell it's a very large fish. After a final strike, he sets the hook—and the fish begins to tow the boat with ease! Santiago realizes this is not an ordinary fish.

The First Night   The fish continues to pull Santiago's skiff out to sea like a child pulling a toy wagon. Still, the fish is a prisoner and Santiago begins to feel pity for this great catch. But this does not soften his resolve to "stay with you until I am dead."

The Second Day   Santiago increases tension on the line to the breaking point, attempting to make the fish jump. The line has been stretched over his back for hours now. He begins to feel intense pain. At an unexpected lurch from the great fish, the line cuts his right hand. And to make matters even worse, his left hand has become cramped like "the gripped claws of an eagle."

The fish surfaces for the first time. Santiago sees he has hooked a marlin "longer than the skiff." By noon his left hand uncramps, and he repeats prayers for success as the fish continues towing the skiff. They are now far beyond sight of the shore.

Baseball, an intense interest he shares with Manolin, occupies his thoughts, particularly his idolization of "the great DiMaggio." Santiago recalls a time in his youth when he too was "the champion" in a daylong arm-wrestling match with a mighty opponent.

The Second Night   Santiago eats a small fish he has caught on one of his other lines, and he sleeps for the first time. Then a furious jerk of the lines wakes him, and his hands get badly cut. The great marlin is jumping. This is good because its air sacs will fill and the fish won't sink to the bottom and die, unable to be pulled back up.

The Third Day   The marlin begins to circle the boat rather than tow it. This is a major breakthrough in the struggle to bring in the fish. Santiago puts as much tension on the line as possible to make the circles shorter. On the third turn the fish is close enough for Santiago to see him well. The fish is enormous beyond belief.

After several more circles, Santiago gets the marlin close enough to kill it with his harpoon. Since the fish is much longer than the skiff, it must be lashed to the side rather than towed behind. Santiago puts up the mast and sets sail to the southwest, back toward Havana.

But a mako shark strikes the marlin and tears off at least forty pounds of flesh before Santiago can kill it. In the killing, he loses his harpoon. Now there is a massive trail of blood and scent in the water, which will inevitably attract other sharks.

And they come. They're shovel-nosed, scavenger sharks—*galanos*. Santiago kills one with his knife that is lashed to an oar; then he kills another, with greater difficulty. But a quarter of the prize marlin meat is now gone. Later, a third *galano* destroys even more of the marlin before Santiago can kill him, and the knife blade breaks in the process. At sunset come still two more. He is unable to kill them but injures them with a club made from an old broken oar.

The Third Night   Santiago begins to see the reflected glare of Havana lights. But the *galanos* now come in a pack. He fights them with a club and even with the skiff's tiller, but they strip the remaining flesh from the marlin.

So now he pilots his small craft home, bringing only a skeleton. He arrives in the middle of the night, beaches his skiff, carries the mast to his shack, and falls into an exhausted sleep.

The Day After   Manolin finds him sleeping. There has been a big stir among the village fishermen over the incredible size of the skeleton still lashed to Santiago's skiff. Manolin tends to the spent, pain-ridden old man and vows to fish with him again.

Tourists look with detached amusement at the skeletal remains of Santiago's three-day battle. They do not understand the nature or significance of Santiago's experiences. Is Santiago a triumphant figure or a tragic figure, or a strange combination of both?

You'll have to decide that for yourself.

The Characters

Santiago

We know he's an old Cuban fisherman. What else do we know about him? A great deal of the meaning of the story depends on your view of him as an element of the story. On one side is the view that he is *simply* an old Cuban fisherman, no more, no less. In that case we have an interesting fishing story, no more, no less.

On the other side is the view that Santiago is Everyman, a universal hero. In that case we have an allegory, a fable, a literary work that consciously attempts to teach us about ourselves and about life.

Outwardly simple, Santiago is really a deeply drawn mixture of many things, some of them contradictory. Perhaps that makes him more authentic.

Sometimes he's a philosopher; at other times he dismisses deep thinking as futile, at least for himself. He entertains almost mystical thoughts about the great marlin being a brother and, in fact, more noble than mankind—and at nearly the same time thinks of how much the fish would bring at market.

He's almost obsessed at one point with sin but reflects that sin should be left to those who are paid to think about it.

On the one hand, he's humble and unpretentious; it doesn't bother him at all that his shirt has been patched and repatched. He's content with little— sometimes no—food. Yet he quietly dares to dream the big dream: to go far out beyond the usual fishing waters in search of a fish beyond all usual fish.

What carries him out and keeps him there is his resolution, a word he himself likes. Call it determination or perseverance or even stubbornness. No mater—he certainly has huge reserves of it. When he has begun something, he will hang with it ". . . until I am dead."

He both rages at misfortune and accepts it. In fact, his most usual posture is that of the Stoic who accepts what happens simply because it happens. "Pain does not matter to a man," he says.

He's full of wistful wishes and regrets and likewise full of statements that wistful wishes are silly.

You'll get to know Santiago very well. He's in every scene in the book except two at the very end, both less than half a page. It's seldom that you get to live with a character so completely throughout a story.

It's not likely you'll forget him, either.

Manolin

"The boy." He has worked with Santiago as an apprentice since he was five. His age at the time of the story is never given, but we can guess that he's in his early to mid teens.

Above all else, Manolin is loyal. Given his long relationship with Santiago, that's to be expected. But more important, he's also exceptionally sensitive: sensitive to Santiago's feelings and sensitive to the pathos, the tragedy of the situation. Perhaps more than either he or the old man knows, he is Santiago's support. The old man needs him.

Other Elements

SETTING

The actual mechanics of setting—the time and place—are easy to identify from a small amount of research. We know the story takes place on the ocean off the coast of Havana, Cuba. An atlas will enable you to locate Cuba and see its close relationship to the southern tip of Florida.

Note the position of Havana on the northern coast of Cuba. By checking indicators of the direction of the Gulf Stream, you can plot the course of Santiago's skiff as it was towed by the marlin, which began swimming against the stream but was finally carried by it.

The time aspect of the setting is equally interesting to track down, although there are few clues. In many ways, Santiago fishes with the same method and equipment as generations before him did. The story would be believable if it were set in the eighteenth century. But some definite references to a more recent time are Santiago's mention of beer in cans and the airplanes which fly over him on their way to Miami. Most obvious of all, however, are the references to Joe DiMaggio. His career lasted from 1936 to 1951, and checking with a more complete biography may enable you to pinpoint the time more precisely by means of DiMaggio's bone spur.

Often the setting of a story contributes greatly to the conflict of the plot itself. The sea is perfectly suited for this and has been the source of conflict (man vs. nature) in countless stories. But not here. It isn't the sea itself that Santiago battles. Here the sea is simply the perfect place for a single man's battle because it powerfully emphasizes—actually creates—Santiago's aloneness. Santiago "on the sea" is a great vehicle for talking about Santiago ("Everyman") "everywhere."

THEME

As often happens in a great piece of literature, there is more than one possible theme. There are many, and people do not always agree on which are central. Hemingway himself said he tried very hard to make the man, the boy, the sea, the fish, and the shark true enough to life. Consequently, they might mean many things to different people. And these different things that people see in his story won't always fit together like pieces in a puzzle. Some of them are contradictory. Here are some possibilities.

Man the Sinner

Even Santiago accuses himself of treachery. He deliberately went out far beyond the usual fishing waters, violating the sanctuary of the marlin. In other words, he sinned. Just as the flood waters of Genesis brought destruction upon the earth as the result of sin, so the sin of Santiago is followed by destruction.

Man the Saint

Santiago is filled with a simple, honest goodness. he loved his wife; he loves Manolin; he loves many things on the earth. Following the example of Christ, he suffers unjustly and undergoes defeat. He experiences his own type of crucifixion. But his acceptance of suffering, again following the model of Christ, inspires and frees Manolin, who will follow after him and continue his work.

Stoicism

Greek "Stoic" philosophers taught that the glory of a human being is to accept suffering and misfortune without complaint, even without resistance. Santiago certainly exemplifies this. "Suffering does not matter to a man," he says. He endures the sustained pain of the line across his back and the cuts on his face and hands. Although he expresses rage at the scavenger sharks, he does not complain to heaven or to anyone over the destruction of his incredible catch.

The "Code Hero"

Closely related to the concept of stoicism is the "Code Hero," a phrase used to describe the main character in many of Hemingway's novels. Some critics regard Santiago as the finest, most developed example of these code heroes.

In this phrase, "code" means a set of rules or guidelines for conduct. In Hemingway's code, the principal ideals are honor, courage, and endurance in a life of stress, misfortune, and pain. Often in Hemingway's stories, the hero's world is violent and disorderly; moreover, the violence and disorder seem to win.

The "code" dictates that the hero act honorably in the midst of what will be a losing battle. In doing so he finds fulfillment: he becomes a man or proves his manhood and his worth. The phrase "grace under pressure" is often used to describe the conduct of the code hero.

Community

Although Santiago's great adventure takes place while he is completely alone, he feels the need to return to the company of others. He is supported by Manolin both before and after the three-day ordeal. In many ways he is dependent on him. Others in the community support him too—Martin, the owner of the Terrace, for example. Santiago knows they will be worried about him. "I live in a good town," he says. Santiago's loneliness highlights the value/necessity of community.

Man Defeated

In spite of being good, in spite of being skilled and dedicated, in spite of putting forth noble and heroic efforts, Santiago does not enjoy success. Even his prayers go unanswered. He ends up weaponless and helpless, a complete victim of forces beyond his control.

Man Triumphant

Santiago comes ashore with only the skeleton of his fish, but he has not truly been defeated. He has achieved a spiritual victory, something far more meaningful than having fifteen hundred pounds of marlin meat to bring to market. Against great odds and in spite of intense personal suffering, he conquered the fish itself and survived the grueling three days on the sea. There may be nothing to sell at market, but the massive skeleton itself stands as proof of his heroic accomplishment.

Suffering

Suffering is both common and unavoidable throughout the story. Santiago suffers from hunger and general poverty. His hands bear the scars of old wounds and they receive new ones. The pain in his back is relentless. He nearly passes out from exhaustion several times. All of it is unavoidable because it results from his being what he was born to be: a fisherman. The conclusion is that being true to yourself and your destiny will bring inevitable suffering.

Good and Evil

As noted before, Santiago can be seen both as saint—even a Christ figure—and as sinner. The destructive forces of evil are readily symbolized by the sharks. If you see Santiago's losing the fish as losing the entire battle, then evil has triumphed. If you see Santiago's endurance and survival as the true victory, then evil has brought tragedy but has not actually conquered.

STYLE

Hemingway is as famous for how he wrote as for what he wrote. Few authors have become so identified with a particular style or with the word "style" itself. Many writers have attempted, for better or for worse, to "write like Hemingway." And the vast majority have failed miserably.

What is it that makes the Hemingway style distinctive? You should try to formulate the answer to that question by yourself as much as possible. Skim back over passages that struck you in particular and determine why.

The essential characteristic of Hemingway's style, in the view of most critics, is simplicity and precision of word choice. See if you agree with that. If you do, find some outstanding examples. What kinds of details does Hemingway give us? What has he deliberately left out that a different writer might have spent a page or a paragraph on?

Another point to consider is the effectiveness of Hemingway's style, at least as seen in *The Old Man and the Sea*. Do you *like* his style?

Let's invent a Hemingway-type description similar to one that might have appeared in the story we're studying: "His head ached truly now. He rubbed it for a moment but felt no difference and stopped the rubbing."

Compare that with another possible version: "Waves of pain throbbed throughout his head, advancing and retreating and advancing once again until the pain threatened to drive off consciousness itself. For a few, brief, futile moments, he rubbed his head with near desperation, massaging his scalp with hopeful fingers that tried to push back the onslaught of pain. But it remained as relentless as ever, and despairingly he dropped his hand to his side."

Which one is better? Or do you have to make the decision? Is it a personal matter similar to "you may like red but I like blue"?

POINT OF VIEW

Point of view in general is also considered in The Story section of this guide because it figures so prominently in this particular work.

Hemingway himself considered first person point of view somewhat more dramatic but extremely limited and said that it took him a while to master the third person and omniscient point of view which we find in *The Old Man and the Sea*.

Even this all-knowing point of view is more simple and direct in Hemingway's hands than it is in most authors'. Usually an all-knowing narrator *reports* what is happening with a character's thoughts and emotions. Sometimes Hemingway does this too: "The old man would have liked to keep his hand in the salt water longer but he was afraid of another sudden lurch by the fish."

Far more often, however, we have what amounts to a direct monologue of Santiago's thoughts: " I wish I could feed the fish, he thought. He is my brother. But I must kill him and keep strong to do it."

Why does Hemingway simply report? What does he expect of his readers? Does he expect too much?

FORM AND STRUCTURE

Unlike most novels, *The Old Man and the Sea* has no chapter divisions. This could be attributed to its relative shortness, but there is another reason. From beginning to end, we are given a continuous account, almost a motion picture of Santiago's three-day ordeal. Until the last pages, there is never a moment when we are not with him. Chapter divisions or headings would be an unnatural intrusion into this exceptionally intimate slice of life.

In this study guide we look at the novel from a conventional framework of time: three days on the sea, with a "day before" and a "day after."

There are other ways, however, of assigning a time structure to the story. The days on the sea itself could be divided into (a) the time before Santiago hooks the marlin, (b) the battle to bring the marlin in and kill it, and (c) the journey back to the harbor. The second section could be further divided into the period wherein the marlin keeps pulling the skiff further out to sea, and the period wherein the marlin begins to circle the skiff and finally is brought in and harpooned.

The Story

NOTE: Hemingway himself gave this book no chapter divisions or sections. The flow of time is uninterrupted from the day before the great journey on the sea to the day after. To help you keep track of the events, we have given this section of the guide the following headings: The Day Before, The First Day, The First Night, The Second Day, The Second Night, The Third Day, the Third Night, and The Morning After.

THE DAY BEFORE

Opening Scene

Think of a time or a period in your life when you were unlucky—maybe unlucky beyond your worst dreams. Unlucky when you didn't deserve to be. Unlucky in spite of great effort or skill on your part. Perhaps it was a series of tests that got bad grades even though you studied. Or many trips to the plate without a hit even though you tried very hard and you're usually a good hitter.

If you can remember something like that, you have something in common with Hemingway's old man, Santiago. He's a good fisherman, an expert. It's been his life. But, as we find out in the opening paragraph, he's gone a terribly long time without catching *anything*. Eighty-four days!

These opening paragraphs of the story are like an extract—a highly concentrated flavoring you might use in cooking. In these opening paragraphs, a considerable amount of background and insight about the old man has been put into relatively few words.

We find that Santiago has had an apprentice, a boy, whose parents have made him work for a different fisherman, because the old man has—and almost *is*— bad luck. So we're dealing with simple and perhaps somewhat superstitious people.

The boy hasn't turned his back on Santiago, though. He feels sad for the old man and helps him with the fishing equipment when he comes in after another day of defeat. If it were up to Manolin, he'd still be fishing with Santiago.

Here you might compare yourself with the boy. Suppose you had played several years of a sport under a coach who taught you a great deal—in fact, everything you know about playing. But this season, in spite of talent, the team is losing every game. People are beginning to say there's something drastically wrong. And now in mid-season there's an opening on another team that's winning. The other team invites you to switch. Your parents strongly suggest it.

Would you?

When Hemingway tells us that the old man's sail was "patched with flour sacks," we know Santiago is not wealthy. But in the same sentence he introduces us to a major theme of the story: he says the sail looks "like the flag of permanent defeat." This concept of defeat and what it means (how do you tell when someone is truly defeated?) will be important throughout the story.

But then, shortly after we see the old and defeated-looking sail, we get a striking contrast: "Everything about him was old except his eyes and they were the same color as the sea and were cheerful and undefeated."

An old saying is, "The eyes are the windows of the soul." Perhaps you've known or met a very old person whose eyes still sparkled, and it told you that the person on the inside was still very much alive and in tune with life. That's what Santiago is like.

And it's perhaps not accidental that Santiago's eyes are "the same color as the sea." There certainly would be other more conventional ways of telling us the color of his eyes, assuming that's important at all. If Santiago's eyes and the sea are the same color, what does that say about Santiago's relationship with the sea itself? That there's a kinship, a bond?

There's certainly a bond between Santiago and the boy, Manolin. And Hemingway says it in one sentence: "The old man had taught the boy to fish and the boy loved him."

This quotation is a superb example of the distinctive style Hemingway is famous for. It's distinctive by being stripped down to bare simplicity, and yet it says so much. A different writer (Hemingway fans would say a "lesser" writer) might have spent a paragraph or a page describing Santiago and Manolin's relationship and feeling for each other. Hemingway uses fourteen words.

Scene Two

You might be reminded of an older person in your life to whom you owe a lot and whom you genuinely love. And you might also think of some times when this same person needed you. Or you might anticipate a time when this person will depend on you for some things—even a time when, in some ways, he or she will be helpless.

That's the situation we now encounter when Santiago and Manolin move from the beach to the Terrace, a restaurant or cafe. The old man has no money to buy a refreshment after his unsuccessful day's work or even fresh bait for tomorrow's work.

The boy buys both—a beer and two sardines. We see the depth of his attachment to Santiago when the boy says that if necessary he would have stolen the sardines.

Note the old man's response: "Thank you." Nothing more. Just, "Thank you."

This is not so much Hemingway's simplicity of style as it is his way of telling us a great deal about the old man. Someone else—a different old man—might have delivered a semi-apologetic speech with things like "I'll make it up to you somehow," "It won't always be like this," and "I can't get over what you're doing for me."

Santiago simply says, "Thank you."

Hemingway explains why. Santiago has "attained humility." He knows that accepting help when needed is "not disgraceful" and carries "no loss of true pride."

This small scene makes a great springboard for thinking about ideas like independence and self-reliance and whether they can be carried too far. Santiago obviously hasn't spent his life sponging off other people. In fact, we'll find that in many ways he's fiercely independent. Yet he can accept aid quietly, naturally, and without feeling bad about himself.

NOTE: False Pride vs. True Pride   Are there times when we refuse help even though we need it? More importantly, if we do refuse, *why*? Loss of pride, no doubt. But Hemingway's Santiago accepts help from a boy because he feels there's no loss of *true* pride, and that brings up a very good question: what's the difference between false and true pride?

At the end of their conversation at the Terrace, the old man gives us the first hint that tomorrow will be different. He is not going to work the usual fishing waters. He is going far out. And he says something that will come back almost as a challenge later in the story: "I am a strange old man."

Scene Three

An author sometimes uses a character's surroundings to tell us something about the character him/herself. The old man's shack is an example. The description tells us that he is poor, certainly, but we also get the impression that Santiago is content with the simplicity imposed by his poverty, because he is himself a simple person, making few demands of life or of other people.

One room. Dirt floor. Table, bed, chair, shelf. That's it. But we hear no complaint at any time from Santiago and no suggestion that he's unhappy. It can't be that he's unaware of any other lifestyle; Havana is not all shacks.

The situation raises some interesting questions. Is Santiago "dumb" for being apparently content with this situation? And, although the book is certainly not a "social issues" story, is it fair for a man to have worked extremely hard all his life and still have only this to show for it? Still another related question might be, Is Santiago in some way "richer" than a man who retires with a healthy savings account and a suburban home filled with gadgets and appliances?

There's no mention of any children, but we know Santiago was married and that he misses his wife deeply. He's taken her picture down because "it made him too lonely to see it."

Now comes a curious contrast with the simplicity with which Santiago accepted his need for help just a few minutes before. He lies about what he is going to eat for supper; actually, he has nothing at all. The boy knows this, and it's likely that Santiago knows the boy knows it.

Manolin goes along with the game, asking if he can take the cast net and receiving permission, even though the net has been sold, apparently for money during a really desperate time.

"But they went through this fiction every day." It's both cute and sad at the same time. Probably all of us do that from time to time—pretend things are better than they really are. But perhaps most of us are not lucky enough to have a Manolin—someone who will play along with our fiction, our pretending, and still be there when really needed.

Into this stripped-down, simple, actually rather bleak existence on the coast of Cuba comes, of all things, American baseball. Santiago and Manolin talk about it in deadly serious terms, as though the outcome is terribly important. It's obvious that to both the old man and the boy the Yankees are the good guys. Santiago reads of his heroes' exploits from day-old newspapers which a friend, Perico, gives him at the *bodega* (a combination wine-shop and small food store). We'll find that even in the midst of his great struggle later on, Santiago reflects about baseball and is concerned about how the Yankees are doing. Why this interest?

One easy explanation is that it's the most exciting thing in Santiago's and Manolin's lives, even though they participate only third-hand by reading newspaper accounts.

But you probably suspect it's more than that. Perhaps Manolin and Santiago are coming at baseball from opposite poles. The boy may see the great players as symbols of what he'd like to be and do; the old man may see them as symbols of what he has done or wishes he had done.

You may find other explanations; critics do not agree about why Hemingway introduces and sustains this topic of baseball through the story, although baseball is a popular sport in Cuba. In one sense it's almost an intrusion, a foreign element. And yet we accept it quite easily, as though it were the most natural thing in the world for Santiago and Manolin to be extremely concerned about the fortunes of a baseball team over a thousand miles away.

NOTE: Figures as Idols   Both of them idolize "the great DiMaggio,"—Joe DiMaggio, the famous centerfielder for the Yankees. This makes a good springboard for reflecting on our own idols. Who are the "larger than life" figures in our lives, and why are they like that to us?

Manolin leaves the old man to read yesterday's newspaper, as he goes for the sardines he's bought. When he returns, the old man is sleeping.

Here is a paragraph to study carefully. It tells a great deal again in the sparing, utterly simple Hemingway style, full of details that are powerful because they suggest so much.

What do you make of brief descriptions like "His shirt had been patched so many times that it was like the sail and the patches were faded to many different shades by the sun"? Do the patches and the fading and the different shades say something about the old man?

What do you make of ". . . with his eyes closed there was no life in his face"? Is it that, with his eyes closed, the color of the sea is shut off—and without the sea he has no life?

Or even the simple, "He was barefooted"? Later in the story we'll find Santiago acting with almost superheroic powers that he finds somewhere within him. But here he's just a tired old man, fragile and, in his sleep, defenseless.

It makes an interesting contrast that we can apply to ourselves. How often we paint ourselves, either outwardly to others or inwardly to ourselves, as completely in charge; and yet how fragile and vulnerable we are in our private, unguarded moments.

How fortunate we are if we have a Manolin. The boy gently covers Santiago with a blanket and leaves him to take his needed sleep, returning later with still another gift: supper. A real supper, not the fictional supper the two had pretended about a short time before.

And this time it's a gift from two sources: Manolin and Martin, the owner of the Terrace, who apparently has done this before.

Remember that we'll shortly see Santiago in heroic terms, gallantly waging an almost superhuman battle. But here he's a very ordinary person who needs and is supported by other people.

Like Santiago, most—perhaps all—of us are fragile and dependent at times, even though at others we act with great individuality and apparent independence. We can wonder who were the Manolins and the Martins behind some of the great heroes of history; and who are the anonymous people supporting the heroes of today's headlines.

Without the supper Manolin brought from Martin, Santiago might not have had the strength for his coming three-day battle. Was there someone who, by some small act, helped George Washington find the courage to lead a ragged attack force across the Delaware? Did someone give an unrecorded word of encouragement that led to Abraham Lincoln's writing the Emancipation Proclamation?

Each of us might ask who were the perhaps forgotten supporters behind our own moments of "doing what had to be done."

The conversation as the two eat supper seems principally about baseball, but it leads up to key ideas.

One is the lions on the beaches of Africa. Santiago really *has* seen lions on an African beach in his youth, and now they're a recurrent part of his dreams. (More on this shortly.) It's significant that the boy does not want to hear about them again. As close as they are, Manolin and Santiago do not share everything, as youth and age cannot.

Another key idea is the boy's comment, "There are many good fishermen and some great ones. But there is only you." After you've finished the story, you might want to analyze Manolin's comment critically. Is Santiago so unique, so larger-than-life that he doesn't and can't represent the rest of us "ordinary" human beings? Or is this simply the hero worship of a boy speaking to his idol—somewhat as Santiago himself speaks of "the great DiMaggio"?

The boy leaves and Santiago sleeps. Then come the lions, Santiago's recurrent dream.

NOTE: The Lions on the Beach   If you had a recurring dream and mentioned it to a half dozen experts, you'd probably get a half dozen different interpretations. And you might meet someone who concludes, "Who knows what it means? You'll have to decide that for yourself."

That's what you'll find if you investigate different critical interpretations of Santiago's dream lions, and even of the beach they play on and the fact that the beach is almost blindingly white. Many experts sound rather sure of what the lions represent. And some say that it's pointless to try to deduce a specific, symbolic meaning.

Here are some of the suggested possibilities. The lions could simply be a reminder of Santiago's youthful days when he too was in the prime of strength. Or they may represent his admiration for nobility of deeds, since a lion is often characterized as "the king of beasts."

And yet Hemingway says Santiago's lions "played like young cats in the dusk." So it's possible to see the lions as symbolizing the great, often violent forces of life somehow tamed, in some ideal but probably impossible world.

That's one you can have fun working on if you like: what or who are Santiago's dream lions? And if you come up with something that you can't find in official opinions but can defend with believable reasons, Hemingway would probably be proud of you.

THE FIRST DAY

Morning

This is the last scene in which we'll see Manolin until the very end of the story, and it reinforces some things we know about their relationship: it's a very masculine relationship between partners who know each other well, yet at the same time it's gentle and caring.

Santiago simply takes hold of Manolin's foot, "gently," until the boy awakes. Once awake, even though sleepy, the boy goes about doing what has to be done.

They are not alike, these two partners walking bare-foot through the early morning dark, but they reach toward an understanding of the other. Santiago apologizes for rousing the boy so early; there is real tenderness and affection coming from him here. The boy on his part accepts what must be. *"Qué va."* ("That's the way it goes.") And he adds, "It is what a man must do." He's accepting a "man's" life, which Santiago has been teaching him, even if he can't fully live it yet.

This maturity from Manolin is perhaps due to having had a good teacher. In many ways Santiago has treated him as an equal, trusting him, giving him challenges. It's significant that Manolin's new employer doesn't even let him carry the fishing gear; Santiago was different. "I let you carry things when you were five years old."

You might stop for a moment and think of who you consider to have been your best teachers. Were they like Santiago in some ways? Were they good because they challenged you, expected you to perform—and yet did so almost gently at times? That seems to have been Santiago's "teaching technique."

Another mark of a good teacher is the ability to teach not just a subject (English, math, Spanish, or fishing) but to teach *life* along with the subject. Santiago has apparently done that just by being himself. Perhaps you've had some teachers like that.

The Journey Out

If you've ever gone fishing very early in the morning, you'll identify with the scene where Santiago sets out from the Havana harbor. If you haven't, and if you read it slowly and carefully, you'll get a good sense of "being there." Again, Hemingway's language is, as usual, extremely simple; there's no lush overload of descriptive words. Simple phrases like "the dip and push of their oars" get the job done.

This is sometimes called "the theater of the mind," a phrase often applied to radio dramas, where the listeners create the scene in their own minds from a few, well-chosen details.

Notice how many sensory details are here. All are stated with the barest of language and often left to the theater of your mind—phrases like "the smell of the land" and "the clean early morning smell of the ocean" and the "trembling sound" as the flying fish leave the water.

If you're up early enough, you can *see* the morning coming. But Hemingway says that Santiago can "feel the morning coming."

Stop for a minute and try to examine that phrase. What would it be like to *feel* the morning coming? We get the impression here of a great event, a real happening, as though the morning is a real *thing* whose coming can be felt from a distance.

And it certainly tells us a lot about Santiago. We know he is no stranger to the sea. But to *feel* the morning coming, entering into the darkness of the open sea? That calls for a closeness with nature most of us don't have.

This closeness to nature is reinforced when we listen to Santiago's thoughts about the sea itself and its creatures. We'll come back to them after a brief note.

NOTE: Point of View   "Point of view" in fiction is not the author's opinion of his/her subject. It's how—actually *by whom*—the author decides to tell the story. Another way to put it is: *who* is the narrator? If a *character in the story* relates the events, that's *first person* point of view. (Usually, but not always, it's one of the major characters.) If the narrator is *not* a character, if it's somebody (never identified) outside of the action, that's *third person* point of view. And within third person point of view, the author has two other choices: *objective* and *omniscient*. Objective means the author tells only what could have been observed by someone who was actually on the scene. Omniscient means the author relates the inner feelings and thoughts of the characters.

Each point of view has its advantages and limitations. In *The Old Man and the Sea* we're obviously seeing *third person omniscient* point of view. You might ask yourself why it was a good choice for this story. In fact, after you've read the book, you might ask if any other point of view would have been possible and why or why not. Would a different point of view have been more successful?

Santiago has many feelings for the sea and its creatures. That's expectable from someone who has spent a great deal of his life on the sea. He feels "fond" of the flying fish because they are "his principal friends on the ocean." We know by now that Hemingway doesn't choose words lightly or just to be cute. So why this word "friends"? "Amusement" or "entertainment" or "diversion" might seem more likely. Is there any way an animal can be a friend to a person? Friendship, after all, assumes something in common, so we can wonder what Santiago has in common with the flying fish. But this much is certain: the flying fish are his guides, leading him to the school of larger fish.

He feels sorry for the small birds "that were always flying and looking and almost never finding." It almost seems unfair that they're doomed to a harsh existence out over the sea.

Here's a chance to wonder if these birds are like (perhaps even symbols of) certain people, because the sea is often a symbol of life itself. Maybe you can think of some people who seem too fragile for the often rough journey through the great "sea" of life.

What's your inner, gut reaction to the word "sea" itself? Perhaps little or nothing; maybe it's a word that has no added feelings or associations (called *connotations*) for you, much like the words "floor" or "ceiling." They mean something but they don't make you feel anything. That's perfectly all right and very understandable if you've never lived by the sea or spent much time reading or dreaming about it.

But to Santiago the sea isn't just a word or a fact or even a thing. To him the sea is a living being with a personality—almost a genuine person, although of a different order of existence.

Some fishermen, Santiago notes, view the sea as masculine and therefore as a rival or an opponent. But Santiago always sees her as feminine. (Ladies, prepare for a bit of chauvinism here—and try to forgive Santiago for it. He is, after all, a product of his time and place, which is a very simple, male-oriented culture.) The old man views the sea with a certain stereotype of femininity: the sea is immensely lovable but irrational, flighty, and capricious. ". . . and if she did wild or wicked things it was because she could not help them. The moon affects her as it does a woman, he thought."

Well, that's certainly not the image of today's totally-in-charge woman, who can be just as good a senator, doctor, or executive as her male counterpart. But we can note that there really isn't any tone of looking down on or mild contempt in Santiago's stereotype. It's an expression of his uncomplicated world view, in which things simply are what they are because that's how they're made. Santiago lives in a male-dominated society.

NOTE: A Personal Reaction to "Sea"   Just for fun, you might spend a couple of minutes asking yourself how *you* see the sea. As masculine or feminine? And—most importantly—why? What reasons, observations, feelings (or perhaps even stereotypes) cause you to see it as masculine or feminine?

You probably won't understand the sea any better, but you'll gain a clearer understanding of your own concept of masculinity and/or femininity. That's a fairly important issue to know "where you are" in these days of debate over unisex versus traditional roles. And if this fictional fisherman can help stimulate your thinking, that's one of the benefits of good fiction. Comparing and contrasting ourselves with well-drawn fictional characters is a great aid toward self-understanding. To make it happen, though, we need to open our mental eyes wider than just enough to "see how the story comes out."

The description of how Santiago's lines are set out and particularly of how the baits are arranged on the hooks is not terribly essential to understanding the plot or the significance of the story, but try reading it slowly to see if you can visualize the details. Sections like these are part of what makes a good story more than just an outline of events.

The same is true of the following paragraph describing the sunrise scene. What do you visualize by the word "thinly" when Hemingway says, "The sun rose thinly from the sea"? An odd word choice. Why? Could the sun *set* "thinly" as well as rise that way?

Santiago is now close to where he wants to fish for the big one that will end his string of terrible luck. And he's doing everything right, keeping each of his lines straight so the baits are down where they're supposed to be instead of letting the lines drift with the current out from the boat, which would make the baits shallower.

This little bit of the nuts-and-bolts of fishing leads him into a brief philosophical reflection. "It is better to be lucky. But I would rather be exact. Then when luck comes you are ready."

Here's one of several passages you can mentally toss around and examine for meaning. It seems strange that he would call being lucky "better," and nevertheless prefer something else. In this case, what he prefers is to "be exact," meaning to do the job right.

Is it a matter of pride—that he would prefer to make success happen by his own efforts rather than waiting for it to happen accidentally? That seems to fit the image of a grizzled old veteran of the sea. But does it fit with his earlier quiet acceptance of Manolin and Martin's generosity?

"Then when luck comes you are ready." Apparently what Santiago is talking about here is not what we mean by the phrase "dumb luck" or "blind chance." Perhaps "opportunity" is what Santiago means. And perhaps he means that opportunities never amount to anything if a person hasn't paid the dues, done the homework, and prepared him/herself to take advantage of the opportunity.

We're reminded of the back-up quarterback who suddenly gets a chance to start. Or the unknown rock group that suddenly have a big-time producer in their audience. Luck? Certainly. But it won't mean anything if the quarterback hasn't already put in hours of training, or if the rock group haven't already made themselves good musicians. Santiago's philosophy isn't too different from the business world's saying, "You make your own breaks."

One final idea before we depart from this reflection on luck versus (or combined with) something else. "Shallow men believe in luck," the American writer Ralph Waldo Emerson said. You might consider to what extent you agree or disagree with Emerson—and Santiago.

Sometimes it helps to identify two opposite poles. One would be a view called fatalism, which basically says you have no control over what happens to you. For example, "When your time is up, it's up," and it makes no difference whether you're a professional soldier of fortune, a race car driver, or an office worker. The same thing would happen anyway.

At the opposite pole would be a view called rugged individualism, which says that you are where you are because you (not somebody or something else) put yourself there. And just about whatever you want to happen you can make happen, if you work at it enough.

What's your view?

In any case, Santiago's ability to read the signs of the sea isn't luck; it's experience. He notices a man-of-war bird circling overhead and he knows from its type of motion that it has located fish—flying fish. They're breaking water, pursued by a school of dolphin.

We have a ring full of contestants in this scene, each with a slightly different purpose but all related to survival. The bird is searching for an opportunity to swoop down and catch a flying fish for food. The dolphin are pursuing the flying fish for the same reason. And the old man is trying to follow the activity in hope that somewhere around it will be the big fish he's after.

In the end, only the dolphin win. Santiago muses that the flying fish "have little chance" and the bird "has no chance." Here we have "luck" or chance or fortune again—in this case *bad* luck. But notice here it's presented as an unavoidable force. Is that because it's concerned with animals in this case, not with people?

Santiago himself doesn't get what he tries for. The school of activity moves too fast for him. But he's too much a veteran to be discouraged. "But perhaps I will pick up a stray and perhaps my big fish is around them. My big fish must be somewhere."

The confidence is apparent. Notice how it's capsuled in the word "my." Santiago speaks of the fish as already his or at least earmarked for him. It's as though there were an inevitable plan or scheme, if only he can carry through his part of it, as though opportunity is inevitable but not necessarily how we take advantage of it.

NOTE: A Consideration of "Opportunity"   Do you feel opportunity is inevitable—that it's always around *somewhere?*

And again just for fun, if you were speaking Santiago's line, "My big fish must be somewhere," what would you say in place of "big fish"? What golden opportunity, what potential prize catch have you thought about recently? To mirror Santiago's situation, it must be something that is possible through a combination of opportunity plus planning and effort on your part.

Santiago jolts us when he literally talks aloud to a Portuguese man-of-war floating beside the boat. "*Agua mala*," he says. Well, that's not so bad; literally it simply means "bad water." Then he matter-of-factly says, "You whore."

Somehow we're not expecting this. It's not so much the word itself as the fact that previously Santiago has never spoken a harsh or negative word about anything. He has come across as tough but otherwise rather mild-mannered.

Yet it fits with his earthiness. And he has reasons for bad feelings about Portuguese man-of-wars: they hurt. They've given him painful sores and welts when some of their poisonous filaments were caught on a fishing line he was pulling in.

But perhaps it's more than that. Perhaps it's not just their ability to cause pain but also the fact that they're beautiful to look at—in other words, deceptive. Would he feel less negative about them if they were as ugly as they are harmful—in other words, at least honest? He does consider them "the falsest thing in the sea."

You could probably make a long list of "Portuguese man-of-wars"—things or people that are harmful, even deadly, although they look, or sound, pleasing.

In any case, we see a delightful picture of the old man exhibiting the reaction of a little kid at a good guys/bad guys movie: the satisfaction of seeing the bad guys get what's coming to them. He loves to see the great sea turtles eating the Portuguese man-of-wars. And he loves to step on them himself when they've been washed ashore, because his soles are too calloused to be affected.

The next time Santiago sees the bird it leads him to a bit of success: to a school of tuna where he catches an albacore that will make "a beautiful bait."

NOTE: The Hemingway Style   Take some time to appreciate the sparse but effective description in this brief scene. Phrases like "the small tuna's shivering pull as he held the line firm and commenced to haul it in" are again both simple and rich.

And what an incredibly, richly accurate description Hemingway gives us of the just-landed fish! ". . . his big, unintelligent eyes staring as he thumped his life out against the planking of the boat with the quick shivering strokes of his neat, fast-moving tail." If you've ever caught a fish, that description makes you almost shout, "Yes, that *is exactly* what it looks like!"

Accidental? Hardly. Hemingway may easily have spent a half hour or more perfecting that sentence. He was a dogged rewriter. (The final chapter alone of *A Farewell to Arms* was rewritten thirty-nine times.)

Another mild jolt: "The old man hit him on the head for kindness." This time it's not so much the concept; we know right away he hits him to hasten the inevitable death of the fish. The jolt is in the words this time, the contract between "hit" and "kindness" within this seven-word phrase. (Another great writer,

Shakespeare, gives us a similar jolt in the words of Hamlet: "I must be cruel in order to be kind.")

Since we've mentioned this "Hemingway style" so often, it's worth taking the time to explore or imagine how a different writer might have said the same thing, in a style much more drawn out and explanatory: "Realizing that if he simply left the fish in the bottom of the boat, its death would be prolonged, the old man hit the fish in the head in order to render it unconscious and hasten its end. Although this would seem to be, on the surface, an act of cruelty or brutality, it really was, in a paradoxical way, an act of kindness."

Well, that's not Hemingway for certain. And it's not effective either.

Santiago is far from the harbor now. He can't see even "the green of the shore but only the tops of the blue hills that showed white as though they were snow-capped and the clouds that looked like high snow mountains above them." Notice the use of color, again in stark simplicity.

He's in water "a mile deep." The big event is about to happen.

The Catch

The next pages describe the catch itself, from the first signal that something is after the bait to the actual setting of the hook. Take special notice of how Hemingway relates it. This section has been both praised and criticized.

It's the very beginning of an epic struggle. Is Hemingway *too* low-key here? Or is his style perfectly delicate?

Santiago sees "one of the projecting green sticks dip sharply." "Sharply" isn't overwhelming, but it's enough to alert us to something nonroutine. " 'Yes,' he said. 'Yes,' and shipped his oars without bumping the boat."

If we're reading too quickly, we could run right past that double "Yes." But it's not an ordinary "Yes." Not from a man who has one sole purpose out on the sea this particular day: to catch his "fish of all time."

He must know something. And according to Hemingway, he does: ". . . and he knew exactly what it was. One hundred fathoms down a marlin was eating the sardines. . . ."

You might check your reaction to see if you're a bit bothered by all this exact knowledge. Some critics are, even to the point of calling it "fakery." How, they ask, could Santiago know that much this soon? It seems to stretch even Santiago's veteran knowledge of the sea beyond the point of believability.

If you have the time for a diversion, you could check with a person familiar with deep-sea fishing (perhaps through the sports editor of your newspaper) to see if he/she thinks it's possible.

There are some reasons for Santiago to logically guess that he must have interested a very large fish, probably a marlin. It is early fall, the time of the big fish, and he is fishing very far out and very deep.

The "catch" scene is drawn out but not too much so. Notice that it has a structure to it, a rise and fall of both Santiago's emotions and ours. Typically stripped-down sentences like "Then it came again" and "Then there was nothing" mark high and low points.

Santiago begins to talk to the fish, a one-way conversation which will resume several times during the story. His nearly childish terms ("Just smell them. Aren't they lovely? Eat them good now. . . .") somehow reinforce how deep is his hope, his almost desperate need, to hook this particular fish.

That isn't so strange, of course. In our very deepest, most hopeful or desperate moments, aren't we usually reduced to the simplest, most childlike language?

Hemingway leads us through several peaks and valleys in this scene; it's a literary mini-roller coaster.

The actual "formal notice" of what a fish we have here comes almost by-the-way, as the second half of an apparently interim sentence: "He was happy feeling the gentle pulling and then he felt something hard and unbelievably heavy."

"What a fish," Santiago says, and it's interesting that at this point we the readers are completely convinced that it *is* a huge fish. By now we've begun to see and feel things through Santiago's expertise, and we trust his evaluation completely.

A bit of Santiago's superstition shows up when he *thinks* that the fish will turn and swallow the bait completely, but he does not say it aloud "because he knew that if you said a good thing it might not happen."

We can smile a bit at this superstitious simplicity, but perhaps we shouldn't smile too much without checking for some bits and pieces of superstition we ourselves may hold to "just in case."

Here comes the decisive, crucial moment.

" 'Now!' he said aloud and struck hard with both hands. . . ." The rest of this paragraph continues with a graphic picture of these few seconds. And when it's finished, Hemingway jolts us again in a reverse sort of fashion with the sentence, "Nothing happened."

Actually, a great deal has happened. The fish has swallowed the bait, the hook has been set; it's no longer a "maybe," no longer a "must be somewhere." It's here!

But the reality sinks in slowly. We realize it almost in a double take when we're told that the boat begins to move slowly off toward the northwest.

The *boat* begins to move? Toward the *northwest*? In the gulf above Havana, that's *against* the current! Slowly, indirectly, through the back door, so to speak, we're given a hint of the great force on the other end of Santiago's line.

Santiago knows what's happening, though. He's a "towing bitt" (see the Glossary in this guide), but he has to be more than just a bitt. He has to be a bitt with a brain, to be flexible and to react to the different movements of the fish.

It's a delicate matter of keeping the line as taut as possible under a variety of conditions. If the fish begins to pull the line beyond the breaking point, he must let the line out but never so much or so fast that the line goes slack. If the fish slows, he must try to pull the line back in if possible, but again without putting tension on it beyond its breaking point.

It's like walking a high narrow plank where a fall to either side is equally disastrous. A too taut, broken line or a slack line (giving the fish a chance to "throw" the hook) will mean a lost fish.

This is quite similar to situations all of us are in from time to time, though usually in a psychological rather than a physical way. For example, when we're persuading or negotiating, it's often crucial to keep a balance between being too flexible and being too hard-lined (the word itself mirrors Santiago's situation). Talk too sweetly and the other side takes over; talk too tough and the other side breaks off communication. Or when we'd like to attract someone we find interesting: playing hard-to-get and coming on too strong can bring failure equally well.

For the first of several times, Santiago wishes out loud that Manolin were with him. It's a futile wish, of course, but somehow we don't blame him for expressing it. We all "wish" things that aren't and can't be; sometimes it seems necessary simply to get it said and out. And somehow we realize that Santiago isn't going to wallow in self-pity. He just needs to say it.

Remember that through all of this Santiago is "still braced solidly with the line across his back. Try to picture him. It's not the image of today's deep-sea fisherman, sitting on a cushioned swivel chair, manipulating rather sophisticated gadgetry.

And he's still there hours later. The fish is breaking even Santiago's expectations: "This will kill him." But it doesn't.

How does Santiago keep up the strain? The nourishment he received from the food—the gifts—Manolin brought is certainly a factor. There's also his pride and the confidence he himself spoke of having. Perhaps the best answer is the words Manolin spoke earlier this morning, words he learned at least in spirit from Santiago: "It is what a man must do."

As evening approaches, he tries "not to think but only to endure." Few of us have been in a circumstance like this. We can perhaps remember demanding athletic contests, but they're not the same as Santiago's situation. It's not only physically draining; it's the *same,* minute to minute, hour to hour. There's no variety of tactics at this stage of Santiago's battle. There's only a demand for the same, nonstop, tense-muscled resistance.

Acute awareness of it can make it worse. Here a human being's highest power and blessing, the ability to think, becomes a curse. Turning the mind off, if possible, helps . . . somewhat.

THE FIRST NIGHT

Being completely out of sight of land didn't frighten Santiago shortly before sunset. "I can always come in on the glow from Havana." But he doesn't get the opportunity. Not this night. Incredibly the fish just keeps towing the boat steadily further out to sea.

By now Santiago has changed his position a bit. He's found a way of leaning against the bow of his skiff and he's been able to work an old sack between the taut, almost cutting line and his shoulders. "The position actually was only somewhat less intolerable; but he thought of it as almost comfortable," Hemingway observes to us.

It brings to mind the saying, "All things are relative." As philosophy goes, that's a very big, sweeping statement. *All* things? If you get into philosophy, you can decide for or against that statement.

But some things certainly are relative, and you can use Santiago's relative "comfort" to think about them. A child born into a poverty-stricken family might look on a single-dip, vanilla ice cream cone as the thrill of the month. Another child the same age but born to wealthy parents might "need" a personal, high-tech, stereo sound system in order to feel that something unusually great has happened.

Wherever any of us is on this "philosophy of relativity," we can at least learn a practical lesson from Santiago. He can't at this point change the situation he's in, so he appreciates what "little" comfort there is in it.

You may or may not see something significant in the mention of Santiago's urinating over the side of the skiff and looking up at the stars to check his course at the same time. It's a good example of a passage where you'd love to bring the author back to life in a totally honest moment and ask him or her, "When you wrote this, did you really mean . . . ?"

At least one critic sees this as symbolic representation of a human being's physical/spiritual nature. At one and the same moment, the old man does something very physical or "lowly" and something very spiritual, at least in a symbolic sense. Looking at the stars and checking the course can easily represent taking a look at the direction of one's life, particularly since in fiction a sea journey often represents a life journey.

It's an unusual contrast of simultaneous activities, and the possibility for symbolism is certainly there. Whether or not it really *is* significant is something you can decide.

When Santiago wishes for the boy a second time, he mentions two reasons for wanting him there: "To help me and to see this."

The first is obvious. The boy could perform the many other tasks besides simply holding the line. But being alone, the old man will have to perform them all himself using his feet and one free hand. This will make rather simple things, like joining coils of additional line, strangely and immensely difficult.

But the second reason is perhaps the greater. For most people, an intense experience cries out to be shared, and a shared experience becomes more intense. A comedy, for example, will seldom bring loud, lasting laughter from one person sitting alone in front of a television set or a movie screen. But the same lines or situations on the screen will bring gales of laughter from a group of people sitting in a living room or from an audience in a theater.

Try to remember experiences in which you thought or perhaps said out loud, "I wish _____ were here to see this." Who were your Manolins who weren't there?

A fish is a fish is a fish. They're all out there only to be caught and used. Do you agree? That's certainly some people's position. And some would say the same about all animals: they exist only to be caught and used for whatever purpose human beings can find for them.

What about animals' feelings, especially when hunted and caught? Do they have feelings? Do they matter?

The next pages contain Santiago's reflections on the subject. By contrast, you might be reminded of the character Rainsford in Richard Connell's famous short story "The Most Dangerous Game." In the opening scene Rainsford puts down the idea that an animal can have feelings (in this case it's a jaguar) and says that it doesn't matter anyway. "Who cares how a jaguar feels?" he asks his friend Whitney.

But Santiago is not Rainsford. He begins to feel sorry for the huge fish he has hooked. Would you?

Santiago gives reasons. "He is wonderful and strange and who knows how old he is." Are those valid reasons or do we have mere sentimentality here?

And has the fish earned the right to die a natural death, rather than a death by human hands, simply because it has already lived so long? (The old man, Norman Thayer, in the film *On Golden Pond* released the huge fish he'd been trying to catch for years after he finally did catch it.)

Santiago respects the fact that the fish is behaving "strangely." The fish seems to have a battle plan, although the old man also wonders if the fish is as desperate as he is.

Then for a second the practical side of the old man surfaces, and he looks at the fish in terms of money. That has to be a thrill; remember the man hasn't caught one in eighty-four days and he has no money for either food or bait. Yes, if the fish isn't desperate, Santiago certainly is. They're both fighting to stay alive.

You might try to think of some contemporary parallels. How about a real estate agent who hasn't made a sale in three months, but now is showing an incredibly expensive, twenty-room mansion to a very interested potential buyer? The commission will be fabulous—if the sale is made. And so the tension is terrific to do and to say exactly the right things at the right time.

See if you can come up with some other comparisons.

But Santiago returns to feeling sorry for the fish. The word for his situation is "ambivalence." It describes having conflicting feelings about something. And Santiago's occupation certainly isn't the only one where a person could have strong, ambivalent feelings about succeeding in his or her work.

We might think of a prosecutor who personally may feel that the defendant is innocent and may hope the jury returns a "Not Guilty" verdict. Yet a prosecutor's job is to do everything possible to convince the jury of the defendant's guilt.

Or a salesperson desperately needing to make a sale might encounter a potential buyer who can probably be persuaded to sign a contract—but who obviously doesn't need the item and can't really afford it.

You've probably experienced ambivalence many times. You'd like to invite a friend to go with you somewhere, but you find out that your friend really should spend the time studying for an important test or completing a nearly due school project. How have you handled ambivalent situations?

The tendency to feel pity for a caught and killed animal is certainly magnified if the animal is one of a mated pair and the mate is *there* on the scene. Santiago thinks of such a situation, a time when he hooked the female of a pair of marlins, and the male stayed with her to the bitter end, even jumping high out of the water to catch a final glimpse of his mate.

Obviously it's the similarity to human beings—the loyalty and love for one's mate—which creates the poignancy in this situation, and again it brings up the question of whether animals feel emotions similar to human emotions. The instance Santiago remembers was "the saddest thing I ever saw with them." Hemingway jolts us again with a sentence full of apparent opposites: "The boy was sad too and we begged her pardon and butchered her promptly."

Ambivalence again. "I really *am* sorry I have to do this, but . . ." Perhaps you've felt it when you were in competition with a friend, knowing the victory meant as much to him or her as it did to you. How often we've heard—and perhaps felt—the saying, "It's a shame somebody has to lose."

A strange sentence comes here: "When once, through my treachery, it had been necessary to him to make a choice, the old man thought."

He's feeling sorry for the fish again, but there's more to it this time. He's putting a minor guilt trip on himself with the idea of treachery, which is a very strong word. Treachery includes the notion of violating a trust.

Santiago is saying that he violated a trust of sorts by going far out into waters where fishermen never go and where, presumably, the fish felt safe from the possibility of a hook being attached to an inviting meal. But Santiago did go there and the hooked bait was there, and the fish had to choose whether or not to take it.

It's as though the fish versus fisherman contest is a rather formal game or perhaps even a war but with certain definite, gentlemanly rules; and he's broken one of them. He has "treacherously" gone into territory which is supposed to be off limits, somewhat like an army sneaking into an officially declared neutral zone and laying land mines.

Has he been treacherous? Or is this beginning to be silly sentimentality? That's your decision. But in either case we learn something about Santiago here. He certainly doesn't feel that "a fish is a fish is a fish," wherever and however you come by it. Not this fish, anyway. This fish is a worthy, noble opponent.

Since he has all these feelings and is aware of them, Santiago comes to a logical conclusion: perhaps he should not have been a fisherman at all. But notice how little time he spends on it. Almost none. Perhaps the thought frightens him or it's too big for him. We find that all through the story Santiago dabbles in philosophy for a moment or two and than backs away from it. He retreats to a that's-just-how-it-is position. So here, almost instantly, he decides that there's no use thinking about having been something different. Being a fisherman "was the thing that I was born for."

Immediately after that he reminds himself to eat the tuna he caught earlier. Within three sentences, Hemingway has taken Santiago from speculating about destiny to reminding himself about breakfast. But that's Santiago. That's how he looks at the world. It's a world filled with things that are what they are.

Now a fish strikes one of his other baits. He knows he can't land it, and it's fast taking out line he will need. So he cuts the line, forfeiting what the fish has already taken and cuts two others, again forfeiting not only line but bait and hooks and leaders. He ties them all together. Now there are six reserve coils of line.

It sounds rather routine until you realize that he's doing all this in pitch dark with one hand, while his other hand is desperately holding on to a fish so monstrous it keeps towing the skiff farther and farther out to sea.

He gets a minor injury in doing so, too. The fish makes an unexplained surge. Santiago is pulled down, hits his face, and is cut below an eye. It isn't a serious injury, but you might try to identify with this small scene. Blood is running down his face and drying before it even reaches his chin. Most of us wouldn't think much of that either; but most of us would have clean, fresh water to wash the blood away with, a germicide and/or painkiller to swab on the cut, and time to attend to all this. Santiago has none of these. He can only let the blood dry and keep holding onto his line. And yet he has "all that a man can ask." What is this "all"? Clear space around his boat (he's brought other lines in now), "a big reserve of line," and the feeling that the fish can't pull the skiff forever.

That's not much by most standards. But it's all that a man could ask by Santiago's. We might ask: What *would* it take for him to be upset, to feel cheated or unequipped?

Santiago's first night on the sea ends with his

speaking aloud to the fish, softly. Somehow that "softly" intensifies what he says: "Fish, I'll stay with you until I am dead."

It's worth pondering what makes this line so strong. After all, we've heard dozens of people, both in fiction and in real life, say: "I'll _____ if it kills me." We've probably said it many times ourselves. But we know that nobody, including ourselves, really means it literally.

But we know that Santiago means it literally. Why?

THE SECOND DAY

Incredibly, the fish at early morning of the second day is not tiring. It's been hooked and has been towing the skiff for approximately eighteen hours. And they're still headed north. Although the force of the Gulf Stream current will carry them somewhat to the east as well, the fish is not yielding to the current.

There seems to be one good thing going. The fish is swimming at a lesser depth. Santiago can tell by the slant of the line going out from the boat into the water.

It brings up the possibility that the fish might be ready to make a jump. Santiago badly wants this to happen. He even calls for divine assistance ("God let him jump."), although it seems to be said rather mechanically.

It's important that the fish jump, even though handling the event will bring a greater challenge. But if the fish never jumps and never fills the sacs along its backbone with air, it could finally die deep down in the ocean, and there's no way Santiago could lift that monstrous body—quite literally a dead weight— up from the bottom.

No, the fish must be brought to the surface, close to the skiff, and harpooned. It's the only way. For that to happen, Santiago has to make it jump.

The way to do that is to increase tension on the line. But when Santiago tries, he finds it's impossible. "He felt the harshness as he leaned back to pull. . . ." In other words, there's no more "give" left in the line. It's already stretched to the breaking point. He reminds himself to be careful never to jerk the line, either. Not only would that risk breaking the line with the suddenly increased tension, but it would also open the cut in the fish, making it easier for the hook to come loose.

Now we get a real mixture in Santiago's next little speech addressed to the fish. It demonstrates how complex his relationship to the fish really is, beneath the surface simplicity of two opponents in a contest.

He says he respects the fish "very much." That we already know. He also says he loves it. And he says he's going to kill it before the day is over.

Admiration for the awesome size and strength of the fish, yes. That's understandable. And previously he's felt pity for the great fish. That's understandable too. But love, combined with a determined vow to kill the loved one? That's strange. Well, maybe it is and maybe it isn't.

This can't be the classic "love-hate" relationship, where intense dislike of certain things about a person can exist side by side with love. And it's not an alternation between love and hate. Santiago isn't even angry with the fish!

Perhaps we have an unanswerable question here, but it certainly invites speculation. Since neither Hemingway nor Santiago uses words lightly, how does Santiago mean the word "love" here?

Because he has talked aloud to himself, to the fish, and to no one in particular, it strikes us as perfectly normal when Santiago engages in (for him) a rather wordy monologue to a small, tired bird which lights on the stern of his skiff, then moves to the line.

It starts with small talk, the kind people sometimes use with animals. Santiago wants to know how old the bird is and whether it's been this way before. The bird, of course, doesn't answer, but it looks at Santiago and he can tell the bird is extremely tired.

The old man assures it that the line is safe for birds to perch on. In fact, it's "too steady," meaning that there is, if anything, too much tension on the line.

Next he nearly scolds the bird for being so tired, since the previous night out on the sea hadn't been windy and thus difficult to fly in. "What are birds coming to?" he asks.

He asks the question in one sense (birds aren't as tough as they used to be), but then he mentally answers it in a different sense, a very literal one. What *are* birds such as this one coming to?

To the hawks, that's what. To other creatures that will prey upon them. But that's part of Santiago's world view of things simply being what they are, and so one does "what a man must do." Or what a bird or a fish must do—a bird or a fish worthy of the name. Santiago tells the bird to rest and then take its chances "like any man or bird or fish."

There's a rich yet simple attitude toward life in Santiago's little pep talk to the small bird. A creature has to take its chances. But chances against what? Well, for birds, there are almost always bigger birds. For fish, there are almost always bigger fish . . . or fishermen.

Against what does a man take chances? Santiago doesn't give us an answer, but you might try to formulate one that fits with what you know of him. And you might try to answer the question for yourself.

Reverting to his original person-to-animal small talk, Santiago invites the bird to stay at his house if he reaches the shore and apologizes for not being able to take the bird there himself. "But I am with a friend."

As in previous instances, Santiago goes from light to heavy. In this case, it's from small talk with a bird to articulating this semimystical relationship with a huge fish. The fish is a friend, a respected, loved friend whom Santiago has vowed to defeat and kill.

Maybe you've had a wound or injury that gave you steady pain which you accustomed yourself to, until suddenly it throbbed and sent out a jolt of fresh pain, making you jerk or flinch. This is what happens to the fish now. The sudden lurch of the fish throws Santiago down onto the bow of the boat, cutting his right hand, and lets him know that the fish is becoming more desperate, feeling more pain.

The old man slices meat from the tuna he caught and, as he begins to eat, realizes that his left hand has become tightly cramped. It seems strange that he didn't realize it until now, since obviously it didn't just happen in an instant. But the constant, unending demand to keep the muscles tensed, the locked position of the hand on the line, and the continuing dull pain have made the cramp come imperceptibly. Suddenly he realizes it's there.

It's not easy to identify with Santiago's position unless you've really had a cramp like that yourself, but it's worthwhile to attempt putting yourself in his position.

To begin with, the cramp hurts. Imagine a great ache all through your hand. Add to that something like paralysis. You command the hand to move, but nothing happens, and the attempt only brings pain.

Before, he had clear water around the skiff and six reserve coils of line. Not much, but it was "all a man could ask," as he viewed it. Now he has less than that, and the loss is not mere mechanical equipment. It's part of himself, part of his ability to move, act, and control the situation.

People who lose the use of one or both arms and/or legs are confronted with the question, "Who really *am* I if I can't walk and handle things and do all I used to do? Am I still me?" In that situation, for a person to survive, the answer must be yes. Thus, Santiago practically separates himself from his hand and in fact talks to it. He puts it down, speaks to it as though it were a perverse member of a team which has suddenly turned traitor.

But he softens very shortly. The hand is no longer a perverse traitor but a teammate again who has been injured and needs some special treatment. The special treatment is eating the raw tuna. That wouldn't be modern medicine's first choice of treatment for a severe cramp, but it's all Santiago has and knows, so he eats the tuna.

What does raw tuna taste like? You'll have to taste real raw tuna to find out, but Hemingway gives us a hint: "It was not unpleasant." Hemingway is speaking for Santiago here, and Santiago tends to downplay misfortune and unpleasantness. Perhaps a truer description follows: "with a little lime or with lemon or with salt" the tuna "would not be bad."

Finally, the hand becomes almost a child to whom you might say, "Now just rest and don't worry; you're going to get better; we're doing everything we can for you."

"Be patient, hand," Santiago says. "I do this for you." The medical care, in this case, is a matter of eating the raw tuna even though it's considerably less than a gourmet delight and Santiago isn't particularly hungry to begin with.

Again, as Santiago eats, comes this bizarre contrast. He wishes he could *feed* the fish because it's his *brother*—and reminds himself that he must keep strong so he can *kill* the brother.

At this point you've seen and heard enough to begin making a considered judgment. What's going on here—sentimentalism on the part of a simplistic old man, or profound philosophy in an unusual environment? It's worth reacting to, since considerations like this are obviously at the core of Hemingway's book.

Slowly Santiago is able to unknot his left hand just a little. Then, suddenly, he has to do something drastic. Because something drastic is happening. Something drastic and wonderful and awesome.

He slaps his hand "hard and fast against his thigh." That's a drastic way to attempt uncramping a hand. But he has to; he needs both hands now. The great fish is coming up. Santiago can feel it in the pull of the line and he can see it in the slant of the line against the water.

NOTE: A Further Consideration of Style   How would you write this scene? That's probably an unfair question if you've never been on the sea and fished for marlin. Still, it's worth considering or comparing your expectations with what Hemingway does.

"The line rose slowly and steadily and then the surface of the ocean bulged ahead of the boat and the fish came out. He came out unendingly and water poured from his sides." If you haven't already, read those two sentences again slowly. Where is the obvious power and drama in them?

Well, it certainly isn't in Hemingway's exotic choice of verbs for the fish's entrance. The core of the entrance itself is ". . . the fish came out." We've been imagining this fish for so long; does that make the utterly simple "came out" effective? We can certainly ask what other, perhaps equally simple, words contribute to the power of the passage.

The following sentences in this entrance scene are equally worth savoring. Note the colors and shapes and motions which are described with beautiful, accurate simplicity.

Santiago has had a notion, a very good notion, of what he was up against before, just from the feel of the weight on his line, and from the rather unusual fact that the fish has been towing the skiff steadily farther out to sea.

The fish is monstrous. "Two feet longer than the skiff." Santiago knows that if the fish "put in everything now," it might well be all over for Santiago. So he decides to try to make the fish "think" that it is up against something more than one single, very old man.

And actually, the sheer physical proportions and powers are a ridiculous mismatch. We know that. Santiago knows that. Santiago can't let the fish know that.

Thankfully, he can perhaps fool the fish. "But, thank God, they are not as intelligent as we who kill them; although they are more noble and more able."

Not as intelligent. That's easily enough understood. People can think, reason, decide; animals can't,
in spite of Santiago's occasional reference to a battle
plan that the fish might have.

More able. Does that mean more powerful? If so,
that likewise is easily understood. The great fish on
the end of Santiago's line is certainly able to exert
greater physical force than Santiago or any other fisherman. Still, his statement leaves us with a lingering
question, "Able to do what?"

Most intriguing of all is the "more noble." "Noble,"
after all, means superior or distinguished in merit or
worth.

Is this huge fish, who can't think or reason or plan
or decide how to raise its offspring, really more *noble*
than the human being trying to catch and kill it? It's
not the catching and killing that make the difference;
fish do that too. Santiago's not championing an anti-
violence cause here. So where is the superiority suggested by "noble?"

This statement won't be the first time Santiago com-
pares human beings to beasts of the land and sea and
sky. The human beings don't come out on top in the
worthiness ratings, as Santiago sees it.

What *does* he see in them that commands such
respect? A certain purity or untaintedness? Since animals can't think or decide, they can't knowingly com-
mit a wrong deed. Thus they move about in some
sinless realm, untouched by willful evil. Unlike people, they are incapable of deviousness and deliberate
harm. That would make their nobility a moral consideration.

If it's difficult or even impossible to figure out what
Santiago means by their being more noble, you can
still compare it to your own feelings or reactions if

you've ever been confronted by wildlife of any kind that gave you a feeling of awe, even if it was only secondhand. (Have you ever, for example, seen the mounted head of a moose and felt, for a fleeting second, "There was a creature better and purer in some ways than the person who shot it"?)

The left hand is still badly cramped: "tight as the gripped claws of an eagle." That's tight. Hemingway gives us an image that we can appreciate even if we've never seen or felt the gripped claws of an eagle.

But he's certain it won't last forever. What else *can* he do but hope it won't last forever? He even comes up with reasons, treating the hand once again as separate from himself, as a member of the team, so to speak, out on the ocean on a mission to bring in this incredible fish. He brings up team loyalty: the left hand will uncramp "to help my right hand." He brings up team pride: it's "unworthy" for the hand to be cramped and virtually useless.

Santiago even wishes he were the fish "with everything he has against only my will and my intelligence." "Only" his will and his intelligence? The statement seems like a crass putdown of what makes human beings human and thus, according to the general sentiment of the centuries, better than animals.

Here you have to decide whether Santiago is talking philosophy again or practicality. In a raw, physical battle, are intelligence and will really useful, formidable weapons against unbending instinct and superior size and strength?

NOTE: Feeling the Character's Situation   It's seldom that you have a chance to really get into a fictional character's physical situation. You can improvise here. It might be called an offbeat way to appre-

ciate a character and a book; it might also be worthwhile and memorable.

Try pulling or pushing against something utterly
immovable, a wall, a huge rock, anything. Keep it up.
Keep it up for however long you want the experiment
to last. But make it enough to acquire the feeling of
nonstop, tensed muscle strain. Are five minutes
enough? Would you go ten? Or would two be more
than enough?

Santiago has been doing this for twenty-four hours
now. And he still has many more hours to go.

There's soon a note of good news for him. Noon of
the second day on the sea, his left hand uncramps.

"Bad news for you, fish," he tosses out at his opponent across and beneath the sea. This is still another
side of his multisided attitude toward the fish. This
sounds like a real opponent talking to another, rather
than a humble contestant speaking to a more noble
foe, which is what he was doing a great deal of not so
long ago.

"There are no atheists in the foxholes," William
Thomas Cummings said, suggesting that even the
most hardened non-believer would turn to God or the
possibility at least of a God if he were entrenched in a
battle under enemy fire. A more recent, equally dry or
sly statement of the same idea is the cartoon picturing
a notice on the wall of a classroom; the notice informs
that in the event of a nuclear attack, the Supreme
Court ruling prohibiting prayer in public classrooms
will be temporarily suspended.

Santiago is not religious. Not in the conventional
sense, at least, although he does have a picture of
Mary on one wall of his shack.

He decides, "just in case," to say ten Our Fathers and ten Hail Marys "that I should catch this fish." And he promises to make a pilgrimage to a shrine, the Virgin of Cobre, if heaven does come through and deliver the fish to him, or at least helps him bring it in.

NOTE: Hemingway's Catholicism The Hail Marys and the pilgrimage to a shrine are, of course, specifically Catholic, which is not surprising considering Santiago is Cuban. And this is one instance in the story where Santiago really is a mirror of Hemingway, who was a nominal or "technical" Catholic. He was baptized in a Catholic ceremony in Italy, after sustaining such severe wounds in World War I (see "The Author and His Times") that it seemed both to him and to others that he might not survive. He remained Catholic, although not exactly fervently so, throughout his life and was buried with a Catholic ceremony in Ketchum, Idaho.

Santiago isn't literally a soldier entrenched in a foxhole, but he is in a war of sorts, a battle which could conceivably kill him. (At this point, it's still possible that the fish could outlast him, tow him farther out to sea, and leave him to die of starvation or dehydration.) And he's at least battling for economic survival—the eighty-four days without a fish. So he prays. And promises a religious act.

Your reaction to this section will depend on your own religious views. Whatever they are, it's worth thinking about. What *is* prayer, in your opinion? Does it *do* something? Does the effectiveness of a prayer depend on the person who prays?

The Danish philosopher Søren Kierkegaard said that prayer doesn't "change" God, but it does change the person who prays. That's not Santiago's outlook. Frankly, he seems to be bargaining, doesn't he? I'll do something for you with the hope that, in return, you'll do something for me. A case of spiritual or theological tit for tat.

If you're quite religious, this scene might come across as a bad satire on prayer and relationship with God in general. If you're not particularly religious, you might still identify with Santiago, the "technical" believer who reaches out to the Higher Power when pushed to his greatest moment of need. Have you ever said a "just in case" or an "I know you haven't heard from me in a while, but . . ." prayer when you were in some relatively desperate situation? If so, why?

Amazing, isn't it, how this "simple," unsophisticated old fisherman can be a catalyst in clarifying our views on rather deep topics?

He says his prayers and he feels better. If nothing else, he's covered all bases, and it's back to the practical and the immediate. Santiago decides to bait the small line still out over the stern of his skiff and try to catch another small fish for food, in case his huge marlin "decides" to stay out another night. Bringing in the monster will require energy and strength which he simply won't have without nourishment.

"I'll kill him, though . . . in all his greatness and his glory." We're accustomed to statements like that by now, these strange mixtures of contrasting elements. It's simply another tribute to the fish combined with another vow to kill.

"Although it is unjust." Here comes Santiago the philosopher again, having just recently emerged from Santiago the nominal, more-or-less believer. What's unjust about it? If animals are meant for the service of people, then doesn't this killing of the marlin fit right into the scheme of things? Or does a great marlin have rights too?

Or does it matter? Santiago, after all, came out on the sea precisely to do this. It's been his plan, his goal, since the previous day. Maybe we have a suggestion here that life is necessarily, inevitably violent. Noble creatures get killed unfairly, unjustly, but that's just the way it is on the sea and on the sea of life. There's nothing to suggest that, even given an opportunity, Santiago would reverse his unjust action and free the marlin. At least not at this point in the story. But be looking for signs that Santiago may change this opinion.

For now, though, it's unjust in Santiago's mind; nevertheless, it's what a man, a real man, does. Santiago again brings in the idea of "what a man must do," re-forming it slightly into a challenge. He's going to show the fish "what a man can do and what a man endures."

Do you think it's possible—really possible—for this one aging, unaided man to bring in and kill a fish longer than the boat he's fishing from? He does call himself "a strange old man." But strangeness in the customary sense of the word doesn't multiply a person's powers.

There's a variety of opinion on this point. Many critics think that Hemingway has given Santiago superhuman powers, such as epic heroes often have, and that there's no way a *real* old man could do what Santiago does.

A second possibility is to see Santiago as a real person whose power has simply been exaggerated a bit here and there for the sake of the story.

And finally, you can see Santiago as completely realistic. Everything he does really could have happened exactly as it's related. He's experienced, skilled, and determined—highly but not superhumanly so, and these qualities make the events happen.

Whichever one comes closest to your own opinion, it's worth considering whether or not it would spoil the story (for you or in general) *if* it could be shown that Santiago could not have performed as he does. The superhuman powers of comic book heroes certainly don't spoil the story for people who read the books. These powers are precisely the essence of the story.

Is that what we have here?

Even if Hemingway gives Santiago a little (or a lot) more to work with than the average Cuban fisherman has, he's going to have to use it, which won't be easy. Santiago will have to prove his "strangeness"—show that he can bring the fish in.

It's the act of proving that occupies our attention here for a moment because Hemingway makes some statements about proving worthiness that critics generally have found very significant.

> "I told the boy I was a strange old man," he said. "Now is when I must prove it."
> The thousand times that he had proved it meant nothing. Now he was proving it again. Each time was a new time and he never thought about the past when he was doing it.

That's awfully strong language. A thousand times that he had proved it meant *nothing?* We usually give credit, don't we, for a person's past accomplishments. We give credit and we give respect to the person, even if that person is no longer able to do those same things which made him or her stand out as worthy.

Think, for example, of aging athletes or entertainers (including, obviously, "the great DiMaggio") who are continually honored throughout their retirement for their past deeds. An acclaimed actor or actress, now no longer able to work, still receives roars of applause in a cameo appearance, even if he or she must speak the brief lines haltingly from cue cards.

NOTE: Being and Doing   The idea that past accomplishments mean nothing is positively depressing to most people. But Santiago (and Hemingway too?) isn't the first person to think like this. It's a view of life which puts all the value—literally *all* the value—on the concrete.

It's not what you are that counts, it's what you do. In fact, we don't even know what you are until we see you in action. Then we know. If you're doing heroic things, we can tell you're a hero.

For the moment; just for now, no longer. Tomorrow you might act like a bum, and then *that's* what you'd be—for that time period. Abstractions are nothing; only the concrete matters.

You need to make a decision about this view. Does it go too contrary to your experience? We do, after all, categorize people. "So and So is basically this kind of person, even though now and then he or she acts in a different manner." That's how we normally think, isn't it?

If we *are* only what we *do* at the moment, that's not a very hopeful view of old age, is it? Most of us spend our final years unable to do the things we did best, and sometimes unable to do anything other than the very simplest tasks. That would make growing old and infirm a matter of growing increasingly worthless.

Hemingway, remember, was growing older and more infirm. He avoided becoming more so by means of a shotgun.

The afternoon of the second day continues almost peacefully. The sea is gentle, the fish simply continues swimming, now at a higher level, and the left hand has completely uncramped. Santiago hurts, of course, and is very tired. That's taken for granted by now.

He wonders how baseball has turned out, the major league *(Gran Ligas)* scores, being particularly interested, of course, in the outcome of the Yankees-Tigers *juego,* or game.

It's impossible for Santiago to think of the Yankees without thinking of "the great DiMaggio," and he soaks up a bit of inspiration from his hero worship of the Yankee star. He reminds himself to be "worthy" of the great DiMaggio, ". . . who does all things perfectly even with the pain of a bone spur in his heel."

That's hero worship all right and somewhat strange coming from an old man. Hero worship is normally supposed to be a characteristic of much younger people.

Whether or not Santiago has superhuman qualities himself, that's certainly the way he looks at his hero. Quite matter-of-factly Santiago says DiMaggio "does all things perfectly." The theme here is performance despite adversity or injury, a theme which Santiago himself is living out.

Another spark of inspiration comes from remembering a time in his youth when he engaged in an arm-wrestling match, one that really was of nearly epic proportions for arm-wrestling.

It went on for a day. The opponent was a great black man, "the strongest man on the docks," and the contest took place at a tavern in Casablanca.

Visualize the scene along with Hemingway's description: the tavern, lit by kerosene lamps; two forearms rigid and straight in the air; the hands gripped tightly, so tightly that blood begins to come out from under the fingernails; the onlookers placing bets; the referees changing, toward the end every four hours so *they* can get some sleep; friends of the opponent lighting cigarettes for him and giving him rum, after which he would try for the kill.

Once the opponent almost does it, too. He has the youthful Santiago's arm three inches off balance, but Santiago struggles to right it, does, and then knows he's going to win. If he can regain three full inches, he knows he's better, stronger. At day light, twenty-four hours after the beginning of the match, he unleashes his great effort and brings the opponent's arm down to the table.

El Campeon (The Champion). He was called that for a long time afterwards, and now, alone in his boat against another great opponent, he recalls those glory days.

Have you ever done something like that to get "psyched up" for a great challenge? Some psychologists, especially promoters of "positive mental attitude," highly recommend recalling a past success, even if it's in an entirely different area from the challenge you're now facing. That's precisely what Santiago is doing right now, and it's interesting to see him doing it long before the days of paperback pop psychology.

Just before dark, Santiago catches a dolphin, *dorado* or golden in color, and clubs it "across the shining golden head until it shivered and was still."

The slant of the line hasn't changed, so the fish is still swimming at the same depth, but when Santiago washes his hand in the ocean, he can tell from the push of the water against his hand that their pace is definitely slower. The fish is tiring.

THE SECOND NIGHT

So is Santiago. He very much needs rest, and although he says aloud that he feels good, it's not true. The pain from the cord across his back "had almost passed pain and gone into a dullness that he mistrusted." That's scary.

But he has gained on the fish in one area: he's had something to eat, and the fish hasn't. And the fish needs considerably more food than Santiago's aging body does.

He rests against the bow of the skiff, looking up at the first stars of the night. They're his "distant friends," a quite understandable description for stars in a lonely old fisherman's night. They're there, and they guide him.

"The fish is my friend too." We've heard this before and of course it's going to be linked up with the idea of killing. So Santiago says it. "But I must kill him."

Well, if a man kills one friend, what about other friends? Kill the stars? Santiago is glad that he and men in general do not have to attempt astricide. Or lunacide. His throughts build to a point of finally being glad that people do not have to think about killing the sun too, along with the moon and the stars.

This section is ready-made for symbolism, of course. What could the potential task of killing celestial bodies stand for? Certainly the idea of impossibility leaps to mind. Is it good, according to Santiago, that we do not have to attempt things that are impossible?

Things like mortality and built-in limitation, then, come across as blessings. Be content with your (relatively) lowly state. Is that it?

Another one for you to decide. Santiago, for his part, admits he does not understand these things and reflects a final time that being free of sun, moon, and star killing is definitely a good thing.

"It is enough to live on the sea and kill our true brothers."

It's another picture of a violent world, a world where "things are simply what they are" and among these things that are is the fact that brothers kill each other. Santiago very simply accepts that condition.

He rests some more, perhaps two hours worth, although it's difficult with the late-rising moon to judge time.

You probably know why he doesn't take the simple way out and simply attach the line to his skiff. He does have a towing bitt at the bow. But he can't afford to take the chance. One lurch, even a small lurch, could break the line, and the great fish would be lost.

Santiago's rest has helped a little, but it hasn't done the job. He could make himself stay awake, yes. "But it would be too dangerous."

He guts the dolphin, finding two flying fish inside it, fillets the meat, and eats half the dolphin and one of the flying fish. It's miserable, but he does it. He has to. And now he will sleep.

The picture of Santiago preparing for sleep is another passage worth reading slowly and carefully, visualizing each detail. It's not easy trying to sleep safely while holding on to a fish that weighs rather close to a ton.

He dreams first of porpoises mating and then, as usual, of the lions on the beach. It's calm, peaceful, and Santiago is happy in his sleep. He deserves to be. He needs to be. One of the great events of the story is about to happen.

Imagine being awakened by a fist to your jaw and a fire in your hand. That's roughly akin to what's happening now. The fish is making a great movement, preparing to jump, which brings Santiago's right hand slamming up into his face, while the line burns through the hand itself.

This moment is what he's waited for, hoped for, and even prayed for. The fish is jumping again and again now, and Santiago's hands are getting badly cut from the outgoing line. If Manolin were there, he could wet the reserve coils of line which now are being used and reduce the cutting friction. But if's don't count now. It's only Santiago and the fish—and the need to "prove it once more."

Over a dozen times the fish jumps, with Santiago giving line each time and getting cut more each time, while trying to keep the line taut. He has to worry about getting nauseated too, because the jerk brought his face down against the dolphin flesh. If he vomits, he'll lose strength, so he washes his face, holding the fish one-handed for a while, and waits for the next stage to begin—the circling of the fish around the skiff.

When he has a chance, he inspects his hand for damage. What he sees would probably send most of us to an all-night clinic or at least to the medicine cabinet. But his reaction is typically Santiago. " 'It is not bad,' he said, 'And pain does not matter to a man.' "

He cannot stomach the dolphin, which he doesn't particularly care for raw anyway; his face was in it, remember. So he eats the other flying fish and invites the next crucial stage in his great adventure.

"Let him begin to circle and let the fight come."

THE THIRD DAY

At last the pressure on the line slackens. Not much. Barely enough to tell. He pulls. Instantly the line goes taut again . . . and then slackens again. Santiago can actually pull line *in*, rather than grudgingly give it out.

The fish is no longer moving farther out to sea. It's circling the boat. A very wide cicle, but still a circle, and that's what the last two days have been leading up to. It's a welcome change, but it doesn't signal the end of the battle or even an easier part of the battle.

Obviously the idea is to keep putting tension to the breaking point on the line in order to make the circles shorter and shorter, finally bringing the fish up to the boat.

It happens, but at a cost. The circles are shorter and the slant indicates the fish has risen. The cost is the black spots now dancing in front of Santiago's eyes. Most of us would find that frightening; Santiago doesn't, but he is afraid of something else: the dizziness and the feeling of nearly passing out. It's happened twice.

As he did earlier, Santiago reaches out and up to heaven with a promised gift of Our Fathers and Hail Marys—a hundred of them now, instead of ten. In return he asks for endurance and he asks for it on credit, so to speak. He can't pray the Our Fathers and Hail Marys right now, so he asks heaven to "consider them said," even though he can't do it until later.

This section invites you again to consider the role or function of prayer in a person's life. So far, Santiago has used it as barter. That makes him rather typical, perhaps. Do you see prayer as serving any other, perhaps higher, purpose?

Now the fish threatens to jump again. It's hitting the wire leader with its spear, probably in reaction to the pain, and the pain may drive him to jump. As much as he wanted this before, Santiago doesn't want it now and instructs the fish to stay in the water.

The circling resumes, but Santiago is feeling faint again, and he can't afford this. A few handfuls of sea water rubbed on his head and neck seem to bring him around.

"It was on the third turn that he saw the fish first." There's another low-key introduction to a dramatic scene. Santiago can't believe how long it takes for the dark shadow to pass under the boat; it keeps coming and coming and coming—all of it fish.

Even the old man, who had a reasonably good idea of the fish's size before, says aloud, "No . . . he can't be that big." He begins to sweat heavily now—not from the hot sun but from a wave of nervousness at fully seeing what he is up against.

Again and again the circles are too short for Santiago to use his harpoon. On one circle he's able to turn the fish on its side a little and for a moment it looks as though this might be *the* moment, but the fish rights itself and begins still another circle.

Another faint spell, more weakness, and always, always the constant need to keep tension on the line. Santiago commands his hands and his legs—and his mind, his consciousness—to hold out. "Last for me. You never went. This time I'll pull him over."

Yes, this time. This time. The fish comes alongside the boat and Santiago gives the pull everything he has in his tired old body, pulls the fish part way over on its side . . . but the fish rights itself again and swims away.

"Fish, you are going to have to die anyway. Do you have to kill me too?"

That's a possibility, you know. The fish, almost certainly, is going to die. It's weak, badly wounded, badly in need of food. But that doesn't mean Santiago is going to make it. At this point he's a rather likely candidate for heart attack, stroke, being pulled over the side and drowning, or lapsing into unconsciousness to die of dehydration and exposure.

He's not thinking particularly clearly, either. Within a few seconds he tells himself he can keep this up forever and that he doesn't really care who gets killed in the battle. Fortunately, he knows his thinking is muddied and speaks to his head again, as he has before, encouraging it to clear up.

Another turn. The fish comes alongside the boat. Again Santiago reaches for strength he is not certain will be there, because he feels himself lapsing into a faint.

The strength is there, nonetheless. But it doesn't bring the fish to its side. The fish swims off.

It really is getting doubtful now that Santiago can make this catch happen, and even he realizes it. " 'I do not know,' he says, 'But I will try it once more.' "

Another failure. The marlin swims off again, its huge tail waving in the air almost as a taunt.

Santiago's situation, the danger of losing both the fish and his life, has passed from serious to critical and beyond. His hands are "mushy," the muscles responding only slowly and incompletely to command, and he can see well only "in flashes." But he decides he can try it one more time.

And one more time the marlin swims away. He feels himself losing consciousness.

The fish approaches, ". . . long, deep, wide, silver and barred with purple and interminable in the water."

Where do we get it—that final reserve of strength in times of crisis, strength we had no knowledge of or even hope for? How often people say, "I don't know how I did it," meaning the statement quite literally.

Santiago drops the line, grabs the harpoon, raises it high in the air (*how* is he doing this?), and drives it down into the fish. And further in and further in, all of his now nearly senseless weight pushing the harpoon deeper and deeper into the body of his brother.

"Then the fish came alive, with his death in him. . . ." What an incredibly simple, perfect description Hemingway gives us here of the death throes of the marlin. The fish too is summoning strength it didn't know it had, but unlike Santiago, the fish will not benefit from it.

There is a moment of farewell, with the fish almost suspended in air beside and above the skiff, the result of its last dying surge. Imagine the almost deafening roar and the onslaught of spraying water as the lifeless body crashes back into the ocean.

It's over. But only for the fish.

There's no great cry of victory from the old man; he doesn't even feel his victory. Instead he feels faint and sick, and he can't see. Numbly, mechanically, he ties the harpoon line around the bitt in the bow of his skiff. And lays his head on his hands. Picture it. It's as close as Santiago can come to a gesture of triumph.

He cannot rest. There's too much work, "slave work," as he calls it, the details of lashing the body to the gunwales of the skiff since, rather obviously, it cannot be brought aboard.

Even in death the fish resists, and Santiago has to pull the skiff up to it. Finally he is able to touch his now dead brother, an act he finds meaningful. Although one-sided, it's a physical communion Santiago feels a need for.

One final spurt of sympathy darts up within the old man when he sees the marlin's eye: ". . . as detached as the mirrors in a periscope or as a saint in a procession." That's another line Hemingway may have spent hours laboring over.

NOTE: A View of Saintliness   While we're here, let's take a moment for the second part of that comparison, the saint's eye. Is it simply a great comparison or is Hemingway giving us a sly, indirect barb at sainthood? After all, he does simply say "saint" rather than "the statue of a saint."

So, having invited you to consider prayer, this strange "little" story invites you to consider sainthood, and whether or not saints are as detached from real life as the marlin's eye.

The fish being dead, Santiago retires temporarily from viewing its mystically and sees it in terms of profit: fifteen hundred pounds, maybe more; perhaps two thirds of that salable meat; thirty cents a pound . . . it's too much to figure in his current disoriented state. But he knows it's a tremendous sum.

If the fish runs only the minimum fifteen hundred pounds, two thirds of that at thirty cents per pound amounts to three hundred dollars. Unimpressive by today's standards; an absolute fortune for one single catch, to Santiago.

The journey back, southwest toward Havana, begins.

Recall how often you've said, "I can't believe this really happened," whether about a misfortune or a great stroke of luck, or just something particularly dramatic. Santiago has that same feeling, and he remembers the moment when the fish was hanging in the air beside the boat. There was "some great strangeness" about it.

At least one commentator has cited this passage as support for the idea that the entire experience has had a mystical dimension and isn't perhaps real. This idea itself may seem strange to you, but not if you reject the story as realistic and accept it purely as a fable.

On the way back, Santiago has to keep looking at the fish to make sure it's really there, that the past two and a half days have really happened.

"It was an hour before the first shark hit him." Here's another masterpiece of a low-key, almost understated introduction to a calamity. It's even grammatically indirect: the "shark hit" comes in a subordinate clause that follows the main clause.

One word contains the foreshadowing that almost tells the rest of the story: "first." It was an hour before the *first* shark hit him.

If sharks can ever be good guys, this one comes close. Hemingway describes it in terms of nobility that fall only slightly short of terms he used for the great marlin. This is a mako shark and, if not exactly good, it is at least honest. The attack is straight and direct; it's described almost in terms of inevitability, as though this is what the mako was born to do.

With one vicious rip, the mako strips forty pounds of the very best meat from the marlin. Santiago is ready with his harpoon and drives it into the shark's brain. He does it "without hope but with resolution and complete malignancy."

"Without hope." Santiago knows what's coming. He knows how this story is going to end. And so do we. "But with resolution." Resolution to do what? The words are probably coming back to you already. He will do "what a man must do," and he will not do it half-heartedly.

"And complete malignancy." For the first time in the story, Santiago hates. As noble in its design as the mako shark is, Santiago does not apologize for killing it. He enjoys the killing.

"It was too good to last." Is it that way with monumental good fortune? How many parallels can you think of from the lives of entertainers, for example, who rise to stardom only to have it collapse? Perhaps there's an event from your own life which parallels Santiago's reversal of fortune.

NOTE: A Consideration of "Defeat" and "Destruction"   Concentrate for a moment on your concepts of "defeat" and "destruction." What's the difference? Is one preferable to the other? In some instances, are they identical?

Hemingway, through Santiago, dangles these ideas before his readers. " 'But man is not made for defeat,' he said. 'A man can be destroyed but not defeated.' "

Do you agree? One way of testing the idea is to reverse the terms and make it: "A man can be de-

feated but not destroyed." Which makes more sense
to you?

Whatever sense you make of it, you can tell this
theme is at the very heart of *The Old Man and the Sea*.
Try to firm up your understanding and position and
be ready to test it out at the end of the story.

Now Santiago regrets having killed the fish. At first
this might seem merely more of the same thing we've
been hearing: it's a shame life is like this, since the fish
is so noble. But this is a different regret. Now he's
truly sorry this whole thing happened at all.

Why? For an answer, you might think in terms of
the meaning of the fish's death. What gave it meaning
before—meaning which is possibly being stripped
away along with the actual flesh of the marlin?

Santiago lashes his knife to one of the oars because
he's lost his harpoon and its rope in killing the mako
shark. Now at least he's armed, even though it may
be a futile weapon in terms of making it safely back to
the Havana harbor with the rest of the marlin intact.
But because a fresh breeze has come up and the sail-
ing goes well, "some of his hope" returns and it
launches him into a meditation on sin.

The initial springboard is his reflection that it is a sin
not to hope. Let's spend some time on this idea.

Objectively, he's right, by the traditional standards
of Judeo-Christian theology. Not to hope is to lack
trust in the Almighty. But only if the doubt concerns
salvation itself, or the power of the Almighty to love
and forgive. Santiago isn't doubting *that*, is he? He's
only doubting the possibility of bringing the marlin to
shore. Or in this story are they one and the same?

Don't think about sin, he tells himself. It's a silly
undertaking because you're not equipped to think

about it and you have enough to do without trying to sort out sin.

Yet he thinks about it anyway, particularly that it might have been sinful to kill the fish. Remember his earlier outlook that being a fisherman and therefore killing the marlin was simply what he was born to do. (Things just are what they are.) In that case, does he have no choice but to sin—since he is what he is and what he does is sinful? Does that make some kind of sense with his next thought, "But then everything is a sin"?

He reminds himself again not to think about sin and keeps doing so anyway. Now he questions his motives for killing the fish. Perhaps the taint of sin is there, and he reflects that his motive wasn't just survival—get a fish to get money to get food.

"You killed him for pride and because you are a fisherman." Now there's an outside chance that a particularly strict view of holiness might cite the former as sinful; pride has often been cited as the root of all sin. But being a fisherman? In other words, being what you are—that made it sinful?

There's not much hope for sainthood in this view, is there? Analyze it; compare it with your views. Is the aging Santiago basically in the same class as the young hoodlum with "born to raise hell" tattooed on his shoulder?

Perhaps there's a way out of this sinfulness: he loved the fish, both before and after killing it. Love for the victim might erase the sinfulness of killing it. Or make it worse, he reflects a moment later.

Good, evil, love, hate. They *are* at the heart of life, aren't they? So it's not surprising, particularly if this story is any kind of an allegory at all, that they're surfacing rather prominently here.

The sharks arrive now, two of them, just as we knew they would. They're not the more respectable mako sharks but *galanos*—shovel-nosed, scavenger sharks. Cowardly, sneaky and very definitely not noble.

Is *this*, perhaps, sin? A symbol of sin? On the one hand they're going to ravage the noble marlin, an act which could serve as evidence for their sinfulness. On the other hand, the sharks are simply being what they are; that's a piece of evidence for the other position.

A much referred to paragraph is coming next:

> "*Ay*," he said aloud. There is no translation for this word and perhaps it is just a noise such as a man might make, involuntarily, feeling the nail go through his hands and into the wood.

There's no doubt about that one, is there? Perhaps it's safer to say that there's no doubt about the reference, the crucified Christ.

Does this make Santiago a Christ figure? There will be some further evidence for this view when Santiago finally returns to his shack in the middle of the night. Many people believe the connection is obvious and it's a closed case.

There's a nagging question, though. If Santiago is a Christ, a savior, what on earth is he *saving* here? Certainly not the marlin. Himself? We'll return to this consideration shortly.

Santiago is able to kill the two *galanos* with the knife lashed to the butt of the oar, but not before they've done what they came for. A fourth of the great marlin is now gone, and it sends Santiago into another wave of guilt.

"I'm sorry about it, fish. It makes everything wrong."

The obvious question is, What's the "it"? The attack of the *galanos*? He has little control over that, and they're being what they are.

It's treachery again. Santiago returns to his previous guilt feelings about being treacherous, violating the rules of the game. "I shouldn't have gone out so far, fish."

Overstepping one's bounds. Does that perhaps tie in with his recent mention of pride—perhaps sinful pride?

NOTE: Applications of "Too Far"   Assuming for a moment that this is the case, let's try to think of some instances where a person attempts *too* much (goes out too far) and in doing so causes harm (evil).

A young athlete who pours his or her entire life into becoming the best, setting a new record—and in doing so wrecks relationships with family and friends: would that be an example? What about a business person attempting too much success, wrecking family ties and borrowing too much money to make the great venture go? Are these contemporary parallels to Santiago who rowed far out beyond the normal fishing waters of the Havana harbor?

Again assuming that your answer tends to be "yes," the really big question still remains: is that *sinful*, morally *evil*? Or just an unfortunate but excusable error in judgment?

There's a practical side to this developing tragedy, of course, and Santiago returns to it. "He was a fish to keep a man all winter." Food versus near starvation.

That's being decided here also, along with all these abstract considerations.

More *galanos*. Half the marlin is gone now. Darkness is approaching and this, we sense, is more than simple lack of sunlight. As John's Gospel notes, when Judas leaves to set in motion the chain of events leading to the crucifixion: "it was night" (JN 13:30).

THE THIRD NIGHT

"Half fish," Santiago said. "Fish that you were." It sounds mildly Shakespearean. He continues with another apology for going out too far. "I ruined us both." This statement invites the question of how Santiago has been ruined. (And was it defeat or destruction?)

He toys with the idea that the fish and he could have been teammates—in fact, *have* been teammates. Together they've killed several sharks: the fish by attracting them, the man by dealing the death-blows.

Is Santiago already dead too? For a moment he thinks he might be. He isn't physically, of course. The pain in his shoulders tells him that. But in another way?

The *galanos* come again, not so strangely around midnight, the traditional hour of evil. Santiago fights them with a club, but a shark grabs it and strips him of that. He pulls the tiller of the skiff free from the rudder and makes it a weapon. It breaks and he fights with the splintered end and then even that is gone.

But so are the *galanos*. And so is the marlin. Is Santiago? Is he gone too now?

There's a strange taste in his mouth, "coppery and sweet." Blood? He spits into the ocean, telling the *galanos* to "make a dream you've killed a man."

It's possible to see the coppery taste and Santiago's brief speech to the *galanos* as evidence that they *have* killed him, that he is actually headed for death from the physical drain of this experience or from some internal injury he has sustained because of it.

This isn't a common view, however. Death, if there is one, is usually considered symbolic or mystical and it invites the question, "Precisely *what* has died?" His pride? Ambition? His meaning? What defeated (killed?) him?

"Nothing," he answers to the question, meaning nothing *else*, nothing in the world he lives in. If anything, it was himself. "I went out too far."

It's the middle of the night when he arrives at the harbor. Carrying the mast (the cross?), he struggles to his shack, falling during his journey, another obvious allusion to Christ. Too obvious, in some opinions. Is Hemingway being beautifully simple here? Or is he playing games?

Whatever, he isn't finished with it. He puts Santiago to bed in a strange crucifixion pose: face down, arms out, palms up. One commentator has suggested that this combination is almost physically impossible.

THE DAY AFTER

Manolin finds him in the morning; he's been checking the shack each day, as we would expect. He sees the old man is alive and he cries.

At what? Evidence of the old man's suffering, perhaps—the hands. Or at the tragedy of it all. Like many others, he's seen the skeleton still lashed to Santiago's skiff. It measures eighteen feet. Mark off eighteen feet somewhere, and imagine a fish.

Manolin brings coffee. Santiago awakes.

> "They beat me, Manolin," he said. "They truly beat me."
>
> "*He* didn't beat you. Not the fish."
>
> "No. Truly. It was afterwards."

The *galanos*, of course. They did it. At least that's what Santiago is suggesting. He doesn't mention, as he did to himself, that it was "nothing" but his going out too far.

"Now we fish together again." That's Manolin talking. On whose authority will he and Santiago fish together again?

Apparently on his own. He's making a break, coming into his own personhood, and he does so boldly: "The hell with luck . . . I'll bring the luck with me." As for his family's opinion of this and of his previous parental orders, "I do not care."

Is *this* the redemption bought by Santiago's (Christ's) suffering—the coming into being of a real person? And, if so, is Manolin the leader now? That's one opinion, although Manolin himself says he will fish with Santiago ". . . for I still have much to learn."

He's crying again as he leaves Santiago's shack. In contrast to Manolin's tears (he alone has a depth of feeling for what happened) are the remarks of some tourists who view the skeleton of Santiago's brother.

They think it's a shark. In that case, they have good and evil mixed up, don't they? They do not understand the significance of these events. They see only a skeleton. They are ignorant of the magnificence of Santiago's struggle.

Of course, that often happens. Even Santiago isn't certain of what good and evil really are and he's not about to attempt to solve the problem now.

He's dreaming about the lions.

A STEP BEYOND

Tests and Answers

TESTS

Test 1

1. The old man had gone eighty-four days
   without catching a fish   _____
   A. and he was depressed about it
   B. but his hope and confidence had not
      deserted him
   C. and that set an all-time record for the
      Caribbean town
   D. but he dreamed that a marlin was
      waiting for him the next day
   E. and he believed that he was being
      punished for his sins

2. One of the old man's fondest wishes was   _____
   A. to make the whole town envious of him
   B. to buy three boats and go into business
   C. to adopt the young boy
   D. to retire to the United States
   E. to have taken Joe DiMaggio fishing

3. The old man's most frequent dreams were   _____
   of
   A. lions on the beach
   B. his dead wife
   C. great dancing fish
   D. great occurrences
   E. contests of strength

4. Santiago wanted to be strong in September   _____
   and October because
   A. he loved the World Series so much
   B. that's when the big fish ran
   C. they all said he was washed up
   D. his manhood was in question
   E. he had been ill during the summer
      months

5. After the big fish took the bait,   _____
   A. it bit through the line
   B. it towed the skiff for several days
   C. it dove straight for the bottom
   D. its fin knocked all of the provisions
      overboard
   E. it bucked and jumped like a bronco

6. The one persistent wish of the old man in   _____
   the skiff was,
   A. "I wish I were back in my bed."
   B. "I wish I had the boy."
   C. "I wish I had the strength of the great
      DiMaggio."
   D. "I wish to keep my fear from this big fish."
   E. "I wish to wake from this night of
      horror."

7. While the big fish was on his line, the old _____
   man said,
   A. "I will kill you dead before this day ends."
   B. "Pull, you devil, I'll never let go."
   C. "You liked my bait, now how do you
      like my hook?"
   D. "It's all very much like a
      merry-go-round."
   E. "This fish will treat me to a tour of the
      oceans of the world."

8. One of the old man's principal physical
   problems was his   _____
   A. failing eyesight
   B. bone spur
   C. excruciating headache
   D. angina
   E. badly cramped hand

9. The old man made all of the following
   statements about the fish, *except*   _____
   A. it was well over one thousand pounds
   B. it was longer than his skiff
   C. it was more noble and more able than
      he
   D. it was more intelligent than he
   E. its sword was as big as a baseball bat

10. If he could catch the big fish, the old man
    vowed to   _____
    A. retire from deep-sea fishing
    B. make a holy pilgrimage
    C. share the profits with Manolin, the boy
    D. drive into Havana smoking a two-dollar
       cigar
    E. buy a season pass to watch "the great
       DiMaggio"

11. Discuss the concepts of good and evil in *The Old Man
    and the Sea*.

12. Sketch the character of Santiago.

13. Explain the roles of the minor characters in the story.

14. Outline the principal motivating forces in the character
    of Santiago.

15. Describe the relationship between Santiago and Ma-
    nolin.

Test 2

1. Catching the big fish was the old man's way   _____
   of
   A. proving that he was a man
   B. replying to his critics
   C. destroying the hex that was upon him
   D. being the "Spanish Captain Ahab"
   E. cementing the boy's friendship

2. Santiago had won the name of Champion as   _____
   a result of his skill in
   A. baseball
   B. riding thoroughbred horses
   C. roping calves in Santurce
   D. arm-wrestling
   E. training dolphins

3. The old man believed   _____
      I. there was no one worthy of eating his
         big fish
     II. that the fish was his friend
    III. that the fish was as old as he was
   A. I and II only
   B. I and III only
   C. II and III only
   D. III only
   E. I, II, and III

4. The old man killed the big fish   _____
   A. by smashing him with his oar
   B. with a harpoon in his side
   C. by denying him food for several days
   D. with a bullet through the brain
   E. by severing his spine

5. The turning point of the story may be detected in the following line:
   A. "I must never let him know his strength."
   B. "Perhaps I should not have been a fisherman."
   C. "It was an hour before the first shark hit him."
   D. "I am still an old man. But I am not unarmed."
   E. "*Qué va*, it is what a man must do."

6. When his fish was being attacked, the old man
   I. killed the first few sharks
   II. lost his harpoon and rope
   III. felt as though he himself had been hit
   A. I only   B. II only   C. III only
   D. I and II only   E. I, II, and III

7. Santiago said all of the following, *except*
   A. "But man is not made for defeat."
   B. "I think the great DiMaggio would be proud of me today."
   C. "Pain does not matter to a man."
   D. "Perhaps it was a sin to kill the fish."
   E. "This day will make me or break me."

8. The old man became convinced that he had killed the big fish
   A. for pride
   B. to keep alive and to sell for food
   C. to keep from going mad
   D. as his gift to God
   E. to help the sharks survive

9. Santiago regretted
   A. having gone out too far

   B. having become a fisherman
   C. not having become a major league
      shortstop
   D. not returning to the cheers of the
      townspeople
   E. ever having seen the big fish

10. Hemingway's closing line of the novel is   _____
   A. "The pity of it all."
   B. "The old man was dreaming about the
      lions."
   C. "Bloody but not bowed."
   D. "Tomorrow he would catch up on the
      American League scores."
   E. "We will fish together; you have much
      to learn"

11. Explain the significance of the sea in the story.

12. Is Santiago a tragic character? Explain.

13. List the principal elements of the story pattern.

14. Project possibilities for the future, based on evidence
from the story.

15. Is the story an allegory or a fable? Discuss.

ANSWERS

Test 1

1. B	**2.** E	**3.** A	**4.** B	**5.** B	**6.** B
7. A	**8.** E	**9.** D	**10.** B		

   11.   Good and evil are portrayed in this book through symbols and symbolic actions rather than through outright, direct actions and objects. Remember that there is the possibility of both good and evil in Santiago himself. Think of some of the good qualities that he displays: his basic honesty, for example, and his obvious love not only for Manolin and his town but even for most of the creatures of the sea.

Yet he accuses himself of treachery, this strange matter of going out "too far." Is that a symbolic sin? The sharks are certainly likely candidates to represent the forces of evil in general. In that case, has evil attracted more evil—and thus brought its own punishment?

12. Santiago, you'll recall, is a curious mixture of dependence on other people combined with the ability to act alone with great courage. His past life hasn't been easy, so he's been toughened, accustomed to hardship and able to accept it easily. His life has also been very simple; his personality is the same. But simple doesn't mean superficial or shallow. Santiago certainly is none of these. On the contrary, his questions and concerns about life are often profound. Even though he uses simple words, the philosopher in Santiago surfaces every few pages. These musings are not hard to find by skimming, and these sections give numerous clues to his simple yet complex character. Small actions, such as his putting his wife's picture on the shelf under his clean shirt and his arm around Manolin's shoulders, give further clues—as do his "great" actions in landing the marlin.

13. "Minor" does not mean "unimportant" in this and many other stories. In analyzing the role of minor characters in any piece of fiction, it's often good to keep two questions in mind: (1) How do they advance the plot of the story? (A character who appears in only a scene or two may be crucial to making something in the plot work out.) (2) What light do they help shed on the main character(s)?

The second of these questions has more bearing on *The Old Man and the Sea*. Notice how Manolin talks to Santiago and what he does for the old man. Then ask, "Why?" What does that tell you about Santiago himself?

14. You might divide Santiago's actions into two broad categories: those motivated by necessity and those motivated by some other, more freely chosen reason. Obviously he fishes out of necessity. Does he accept this necessity? What other things does he do because "it is what a man must do"?

But he doesn't have to go out as far as he does. Why *does* he? Pure financial gain (a huge catch to make up for his eighty-four fishless days) is one possibility. There may be others, however. Is he trying to prove something? To himself, or to others?

15. It's helpful here to note areas in which Santiago and Manolin *need* each other and areas in which they *choose* each other. The need is not difficult to define. Manolin will be a fisherman; he needs someone to teach him the trade, a trade which is not nearly so simple as it may seem. Santiago's need for the boy is well documented in the opening pages, where Manolin literally supplies food the old man needs. But it's overwhelmingly obvious that this is not a mere business arrangement. There's also a teacher–student relationship, but it's far more than that too. The boy loves Santiago. But only because the old man had taught him to fish?

There's only one reference to the boy's actual father. It's certainly feasible to conclude that the father is as absent from Manolin as he virtually is from the story. Santiago seems to be a greater paternal force.

Test 2

1. A   **2.** D   **3.** A   **4.** B   **5.** C   **6.** E

7. E   **8.** A   **9.** A   **10.** B

11. Almost simplistically, the sea provides the setting. Without it, there would be no story. But it's much more than that. The sea is the biggest *thing* both in type and in area that we have here on earth. Confronted with the vast expanse of the sea, a person nearly always experiences a "bigger than me" feeling. Consequently, the sea has often been used in fiction as a symbol of life or the mother of life.

A journey on the sea is often, in fiction, a symbolic journey through life, with all the accompanying things and events likewise acquiring symbolic significance. Santiago, as many people before and after him, sees the sea as living and personal.

12. The viewpoint here depends upon one's definition of tragedy and tragic characters. If "tragedy" is taken in a more common sense to mean simply a person to whom bad things happen, then certainly he's supremely qualified.

But sometimes "tragic" is used in literature in a more narrow sense to describe a character who comes to an unfortunate end because of some flaw in his or her character. In this case, the prime suspect is Santiago for going out "too far," which can be taken to mean various forms of sinfulness. The source of defeat, then, is from within. Santiago himself mentions the possibility. Do you accept this possibility?

13. A story pattern is classically composed of these elements: **introduction** or exposition, which sets the scene; **rising action,** an initial, complicating event which begins the conflict followed by a series of events (sometimes called "crises") that heighten it; a **climax,** in which the conflict is resolved; and the **denouement** or falling action, which concludes the story.

The Old Man and the Sea follows this pattern with precision. **Introduction:** Santiago and Manolin talk and prepare for the following morning. **Rising action:** Santiago's three days on the sea are filled with an increasing series of events which raise the tension. **Climax:** The marlin is finally destroyed by the sharks. **Denouement:** Santiago struggles to his shack and is found by the boy.

Our story also includes two other "optional" elements of a classic story pattern: **foreshadowing,** a suggestion or hint of what is to come or what might come; **technical climax,** a point at which the outcome of the story seems apparent to the reader, even though it hasn't happened yet. Skim the story to find your choice for this technical climax. At what point do *you* feel it becomes apparent that sharks will destroy the marlin?

14. (a) Santiago will die as a result of the terrible strain and some injury sustained during his experience.

(b) Santiago will recover; he and Manolin will fish together again.

(c) Santiago will recover, but he and Manolin will not be a team again.

15. Hemingway's much-quoted explanation about making "a real old man, a real boy, a real sea, and a real fish and a real shark" originally appeared in *Time*, December 13, 1954 (Pacific edition). He added: "But if I make them good and true enough, they would mean many things."

This seems like an open admission that the story is an allegorical piece except for the word "many." We frequently want a fable to mean a single, agreed upon, definite thing, as though sufficient study of the text would produce an inescapable single moral or lesson. That may be true of Aesop, but it certainly isn't true of Hemingway in *The Old Man and the Sea*.

It doesn't have to be, either. And there are many qualities of this story which make it ripe for being interpreted as an allegory. One is the singleness, the aloneness of the main character, who operates entirely by himself through 80 percent of the story's pages. Another, as we've mentioned before, is the setting: the vast, mysterious sea.

Term Paper Ideas

Good/Evil

1. Santiago (perhaps representing mankind) is a good, even saintly person in his own way.

2. Santiago, like all of us, is a sinner and suffers the consequences of his sin.

3. Santiago's basic sin was that of pride: wanting to accomplish too much.

4. The forces of evil in life are both powerful and unavoidable. (Santiago is virtually helpless against the sharks.)

5. Evil triumphs in the end. (The marlin is destroyed.)

6. Evil can cause harm and suffering but cannot ultimately triumph. Santiago's courage allows him to prevail.

Suffering

1. Suffering is unavoidable because it comes from being what you are.

2. Suffering is necessary to prove one's worth.

3. Suffering brings redemption or salvation.

Defeat/Victory

1. Santiago has been defeated by the sharks but has not been destroyed as a person.

2. Santiago has been destroyed by the experience (he may die or be unable to fish again) but has not been truly defeated.

3.   Santiago has been both defeated and destroyed by the experience.

4.   The human spirit can endure anything through sheer willpower and thus emerge with at least a spiritual victory.

Prayer/Relationship with God

1.   Prayer does not accomplish anything; it changes neither God nor the person praying.

2.   Prayer accomplishes nothing if it is mechanical and used only to barter with God.

3.   Prayers for a purely selfish concern are not answered.

4.   God often answers prayers in a different way. (Santiago did not come home with the fish, but he did survive.)

Love/Community

1.   People need and depend on each other; without each other, we cannot survive.

2.   Love is the most powerful of forces.

3.   We share a mysterious kinship with every created thing: other people, animals, even objects in the universe such as stars.

Loneliness

1.   Loneliness in old age is inevitable, as Santiago says.

2.   In loneliness a person finds what he or she is really capable of doing.

3. Loneliness provides time to think and learn who you really are.

Justice/Injustice

1. It is unfair that Santiago (or anyone in similar circumstances) should have to battle alone.

2. Life is harsh but just; in the end, Santiago is justly punished.

3. Life is harsh and unjust; like so many people before and after him, Santiago does not receive the due reward of his labor.

4. Santiago's poverty is a social concern that the community should do something about.

Manolin

1. Manolin's character: he is loyal, loving, and caring.

2. Manolin's apprenticeship: he has learned many things from the old man—about life, as well as about fishing.

3. Manolin is *too* loyal and dedicated to be believable.

Santiago

1. Santiago is/is not appropriate as a central figure in an allegory.

2. Santiago as teacher: what and how has he taught the boy?

3. Discuss Santiago as father. (He commands more loyalty than the boy's real father.)

Old Age

1. Old age can be a friend to youth; the generation gap does not have to exist.

2. Old age can bring life's greatest triumphs.

3. Old age is a curse.

4. Old age is a richness of experience and wisdom.

Miscellaneous

1. A life lived close to nature, as Santiago's, is both simpler and richer than life in a technological society.

2. Technology can conquer or at least control the forces of nature.

Further Reading

CRITICAL WORKS

Atkins, John. *The Art of Ernest Hemingway*. London: 1952, pp. 244–247.

Baker, Carlos. *Ernest Hemingway: A Life Story*. New York: 1969, pp. 501–507. (This book is considered the authoritative biography.)

Baker, Sheridan. *Ernest Hemingway: An Introduction and Interpretation*. New York: 1967, pp. 126–136.

Burgess, Anthony. *Ernest Hemingway and His World*. New York: 1979.

Burhans, Clinton S. "*The Old Man and the Sea*: Hemingway's Tragic Vision of Man," in *Hemingway and His Critics*. New York, 1961, pp. 259–268.

Donaldson, Scott. *By Force of Will: The Life in Art and Art in the Life of Ernest Hemingway*. New York, 1977.

Harada, Keiichi. "The Marlin and the Shark: A Note on *The Old Man and the Sea*," in *Hemingway and His Critics*. New York: 1961, pp. 269–276.

Jobes, Katherine T. *Twentieth Century Interpretations of "The Old Man and the Sea."* Englewood Cliffs: 1968. A collection of nineteen essays on the book.

Shaw, Samuel. "Lions on the Beach," in *Ernest Hemingway*. New York: 1973, pp. 114–118.

Waldhorn, Arthur. *A Reader's Guide to Ernest Hemingway*. New York: 1972.

Williams, Wirt. *The Tragic Art of Ernest Hemingway*. Baton Rouge: 1981.

Wylder, Delbert E. "The Hero as Saint and Sinner," in *Hemingway's Heroes*. Albuquerque: 1969, pp. 199–222.

AUTHOR'S OTHER WORKS

Glossary

Bitt A post on the deck of a boat, usually with a rope attached, used either to secure the boat or to tow it.

Bonito, albacore Types of fish of the tuna family.

Bow The front end of a boat. (The back is the *stern*.)

Bringing a fish in too green Attempting to get a fish into the boat when it has too much life and strength left.

Brisa Breeze.

Calambre Cramp.

Cast net A usually round, weighted net designed to be thrown downward and then pulled back by strings. Used for catching small bait fish.

Dentuso Having big teeth, "toothy"; a sort of nickname Santiago uses for the shark.

Dorado Golden.

Espuela de hueso A bone spur.

Fathom Six feet. Thus, Santiago's baits range from 240 to 750 feet deep.

Flying fish A fish with a long pectoral fin which can look like a wing. After getting up a burst of speed, the fish can leave the water and move through the air for several feet.

Gaff A large, sharp hook at the end of a rod or pole, used to help pull a large fish from the water.

Harpoon A barbed spear with a rope attached.

Hawk-bills A deep-sea turtle; their shells are brown mottled with yellow and are quite valuable. Usually spelled hawksbill.

Juego Game or sport.

Loggerheads A large, deep-sea turtle, not as attractive nor as valuable as hawksbill turtles.

Plankton Tiny plants and animals that float in a body of water; the main food source for aquatic animals.

Portuguese man-of-war A jellyfish-like creature that floats on the surface of the sea, with tiny stinging organs which can cause painful, sometimes serious injury.

Qué va Can mean many things in different contexts; as used herein, it means something like "that's how it goes" or "that's life" or "whatever happens will happen."

Salac A Cuban colloquial word meaning touched or even cursed by bad luck and therefore able to spread it; the bad luck is contagious.

Sargasso weed, Gulf weed Types of seaweed.

Skiff A small, light boat. Santiago's skiff is propelled by oars and sail.

Thole pins Pegs set into the upper edges of the side of a boat (the gunwales); the oars are attached to these.

Thwart The seat, usually just a wide board which extends from side to side at the middle of the boat.

The Critics

The Novel as a Whole

The last "novel" to be published during Hemingway's lifetime was *The Old Man and the Sea*, a work which Hemingway would identify as a new form. The precise generic classification is more or less inconsequential, although it is apparent that the work is a completely developed fable in the form of a very short novel.

> —Delbert E. Wylder, in *Hemingway's Heroes*.

The secret about the novel, Ernest explained, was that there wasn't any symbolism. Sea equaled sea, old man was old man, the boy was a boy, the marlin was itself, and the sharks were no better and no worse than other sharks.

> —Carlos Baker, *Ernest Hemingway*.

Indeed, the critical reception of the novel has emphasized this (metaphorical) aspect of it: in particular, Philip Young, Leo Gurko, and Carlos Baker have stressed the qualities of *The Old Man and the Sea* as allegory and parable.

> —Clinton S. Burhans, in *Hemingway and His Critics*.

Santiago as Saint/Sinner

Before the old fisherman is himself identified by obvious allusion with the crucified Christ, he is identified with Cain and with the crucifiers of Christ.

> —Arvin P. Wells, in *Twentieth Century Interpretations*.

The protagonist of the book brings to full circle Hemingway's use of the mythic hero, for Santiago is again a hero with a different face. He is a modern adaptation of . . . the saint or ascetic.

> —Delbert E. Wylder, in *Hemingway's Heroes*.

Santiago as Christ Figure

One may wonder whether the Christ image is entirely appropriate. It would appear that it reinforces the thrust of the book of Christ as conceived in his human aspect only. The *suffering* Christ is consistent with Hemingway's tragic vision.

> —Samuel Shaw, in *Ernest Heming-*
> *way*.

Moreover, there are suggestions of Calvary . . . in the old man's struggling up the hill and falling under the weight of his mast, and further suggestions of the Crucifixion.

> —Carlos Baker, *Ernest Hemingway*.

Santiago's Dream Lions

The "lions on the beach" have been variously interpreted. The reader may permit himself the widest latitude without going wrong or doing violence to the words—a dream of adventure, of boundless energy and pride, of love for the universe, of the million bounties of life. It is a phrase whose general meaning is clear but in which each man may find something special for himself.

> —Samuel Shaw, in *Ernest Heming-*
> *way*.

A Negative View

This hint that Hemingway may be padding his characterization of Santiago by means of fakery is abundantly confirmed by the action that follows. His combat with the fish is an ordeal that would do in even a vigorous young man.

> —Robert P. Weeks, in *Twentieth Cen-*
> *tury Interpretations*.